A Guide to Tribal Ownership of a National Bank

Washington, DC
September 2002

This guide, prepared by the Office of the Comptroller of the Currency (OCC), is intended to provide an introduction to tribal ownership of national banks. The OCC encourages tribes and national banks to consult with counsel familiar with banking law, federal Indian law, and tribal law, as appropriate, to obtain specific advice on chartering, acquiring, or operating a national bank.

A Guide to Tribal Ownership of a National Bank

Table of Contents

A Guide to Tribal Ownership of a National Bank

Background

This guide is intended to assist federally recognized Indian tribes in exploring entry into the national banking system by establishing or acquiring control of a national bank. Specifically, it:

- Provides background information to consider when entering banking.

- Outlines the Office of the Comptroller of the Currency's (OCC's) corporate application process.

- Summarizes supervision and oversight of national banks.

- Addresses operational issues relevant to tribally owned banks.

- Includes a glossary and a reference section, listing additional OCC publications and other resources.

Preliminary Considerations

Before a tribal government decides to invest in a financial institution, it should consider whether a financial institution is the best organizational structure to achieve its objectives. To reach this decision, a tribe may want to consult with legal, financial, and business advisors. Alternatives to owning a financial institution could include creating a nonbank entity (e.g., a finance company or loan fund), a community development corporation (CDC), a small business investment company, or partnerships with existing financial institutions. Some of these structures may be used in conjunction with the establishment or acquisition of a tribally owned financial institution.

Types of Charters

Financial Institutions

A tribal government interested in starting its own financial institution must first determine the type of charter that best suits its objectives. The most common charters are: national or state bank, federal or state savings association, federal or state savings bank, and federal or state credit union. Each charter offers different benefits. Appendix A lists the regulatory agency that has licensing and primary regulatory authority for each charter.

The banking industry is regulated closely because financial institutions are important to the economy and enjoy government-sponsored benefits, particularly federal deposit insurance. Banking laws govern the activities in which institutions may engage, and bank regulators monitor those activities closely to ensure that institutions conduct them in a safe and sound manner and without undue risk to the Federal Deposit Insurance Fund. Each potential entrant into banking must work closely with appropriate federal or state regulators to meet legal, policy, and procedural requirements.

National Banks

National banks are chartered by the OCC and are distinguished by the word "national" or the initials "N.A." (national association) in their formal titles. They have many attributes. For example, they have broad lending authority and the ability to engage directly in a wide range of financial services activities. In addition, national banks have the advantage of operating under the primary supervision of one regulatory agency. They also enjoy a strong reputation resulting from the high standards set by federal law and regulations.

The primary federal regulator of national banks is the Office of the Comptroller of the Currency. The OCC charters, regulates, and supervises national banks and federal branches and agencies of foreign banks in the United States. Those institutions account for more than half of the nation's banking assets. The OCC's mission is to ensure a safe, sound, and competitive national banking system that supports the citizens, communities, and economy of the United States.

Indian Tribes Owning Financial Institutions

Tribal Sovereignty

Since its formation, the United States has acknowledged the status of federally recognized Indian tribes[1] as "domestic dependent nations" that exercise governmental authority over their members and their territory.[2] In numerous treaties and agreements, the United States has guaranteed the right of Indian tribes to self-government[3] and pledged to protect Indian tribes. Congress has

---

[1] "Indian Entities Recognized and Eligible to Receive Services from the United States Bureau of Indian Affairs," 67 Fed. Reg. 46,328 (July 12, 2002).

[2] In Oklahoma Tax Comm'n v. Citizen Band of Potawatomi Indian Tribe, 498 U.S. 505, 509 (1991), the Supreme Court explained that "Indian tribes are 'domestic dependent nations' that exercise inherent sovereignty over their members and territories." Id. (quoting) Cherokee Nation v. Georgia, 30 U.S. (5 Pet.) 1, 17 (1831). As "domestic dependent nations," Indian tribes have authority to, among other things, determine the form of tribal government; determine tribal membership; maintain law and order; administer justice; levy taxes; license, and regulate activities on Indian lands; regulate domestic relations; and promote tribal economic development. See generally, F. Cohen, Handbook of Federal Indian Law at 246-57 (1982 ed.); 25 USC 476-477 (Indian Reorganization Act).

[3] In Ex Parte Crow Dog, 109 U.S. 556, 568-69 (1883), for example, the Supreme Court explained that

---

recognized that "the United States has a trust responsibility to [Indian tribes] that includes the protection of the sovereignty of each tribal government."[4] As directed in the presidential executive order on "Consultation and Coordination with Indian Tribal Governments" dated November 6, 2000, the OCC recognizes tribal sovereignty and works with every federally recognized Indian tribe on a government-to-government basis.

Legal and Practical Considerations

Financial institutions that engage in interstate commerce must comply with applicable federal and state banking laws, including chartering requirements. Given the nature of the United States financial system, all banks operating in this country are engaged in interstate commerce. Therefore, any Indian tribe that plans to create a depository institution must obtain a federal or state charter. In addition, each tribe must review its tribal law to confirm that it does not preclude the tribe from owning a depository institution. The following legal and practical considerations also require that an Indian tribe obtain either a federal or state charter to create a depository institution.

Deposit Insurance

The success of any depository institution depends largely on its customers' confidence in the institution's ability to repay their deposits. Federal deposit insurance ensures customers that their funds are safe. Therefore, an institution offering federal deposit insurance can maintain a stable base of deposits, which is critical to funding the institution's lending business and other activities. Under federal law,[5] deposit insurance is available only to financial institutions that have a federal or state charter.

Legal Restrictions

Federal law places severe restrictions on depository institutions that do not have federal deposit insurance. For example, such uninsured entities:

- Must agree to be examined by state banking regulators in order to take deposits (12 USC 378).

---

under the Treaty of 1868 with the Sioux, "among the arts of civilized life, which it was the very purpose of all these arrangements to introduce and naturalize among [the Indians], was the highest and best of all, that of self-government." Earlier, in the seminal case Worcester v. Georgia, 31 U.S. (6 Pet.) 515, 555-56 (1832), the Court had ruled that the Treaty of Holston "recogniz[ed] the national character of the Cherokees, and their right of self-government."

[4] 25 USC 3601(2); see also 25 USC 450, 1451, 1601, 2501-2, 3701, and 4101.

[5] 12 USC 1813, 1815; 12 USC 1781.

- Must disclose to customers their lack of federal deposit insurance before taking deposits (12 USC 1831t(b)).

- Generally may not receive deposits through the mail (12 USC 1831t(e)).

Further, because of potential confusion over the regulated nature of a financial institution, federal criminal law prohibits use of the words "national," "Federal," "United States," "reserve," or "Deposit Insurance" in the names of institutions engaged in certain financial businesses (18 USC 709). In addition, federal laws regarding disclosure of financial transactions (e.g., those requiring disclosure of income to the Internal Revenue Service or large cash transactions to the Treasury Department) apply to all businesses within the United States, even if the transactions occur in Indian country.

Business Relationships

A financial institution's success also results from the willingness of other institutions to join it in correspondent and other business relationships. For example, several payments systems for wire transfers and check clearing in the United States are organized and operated by federally and state-chartered insured depository institutions or the Board of Governors of the Federal Reserve System (FRB). Access to those systems generally is limited to institutions that are federally insured and examined regularly by federal or state regulators for safety and soundness. This ability to enter into reciprocal clearing and payment relationships gives federally or state-chartered banks a greater opportunity to provide necessary financial services to their communities.

Getting Started

A tribal government that decides to charter or acquire a national bank should contact the OCC's Licensing staff to obtain guidance and technical assistance before beginning the licensing process. (See Appendix F for a listing of the appropriate district office and Washington headquarters contacts.)

This guide provides cross-references to the *Comptroller's Licensing Manual* (licensing manual), which sets out the licensing procedures. Those booklets, which include sample forms, may be obtained from the OCC's Communications Division. They are also available on the OCC's Web site at http://www.occ.treas.gov. Appendix G provides instructions on how to obtain the booklets.

This guide also addresses issues raised in the licensing and supervision processes that have been common to previous tribal applicants. Indian tribes should consider them in the context of their own tribal laws and economic goals. The OCC recognizes that, as domestic dependent nations, tribes may have different perspectives and invites potential tribal applicants to offer new or alternative solutions to these issues.

Finally, the OCC respects the important Native American traditions and cultures that may emerge in business relationships with tribes and tribal members. To the extent that those cultural issues affect the corporate application process, the OCC encourages tribal applicants to discuss them with the Licensing staff to work through any issues they may present.

A tribe can enter the national banking system by:

- Establishing a new national bank charter.

- Acquiring a national bank through a merger transaction.

- Acquiring the stock of an existing national bank.

- Converting an existing institution to a national bank.

A national bank may be owned directly by a tribe or group of tribes or through a bank holding company (BHC) that is owned by a tribe or group of tribes.

New National Bank Charter

The OCC approves proposals to establish national banks that will foster healthy competition, operate in a safe and sound manner, and have a reasonable chance of success. In so doing, the OCC does not guarantee that a proposal to establish a national bank is without risk to the organizers or investors. Each applicant must publish a notice of application in a newspaper of general circulation in the community in which the proposed bank will be located. The public may submit comments during this notice period. (See the "Charters" booklet of the licensing manual for a complete discussion of the chartering process and the "Public Involvement" booklet for a discussion of the public's role in this process.)

Decision Criteria

In reaching its decision, the OCC considers whether the proposed bank:

- Has organizers who are familiar with national banking laws and regulations.

- Has competent management, including a board of directors, that has the ability and experience relevant to the type of services to be provided.

- Has capitalization that is sufficient to support the projected volume and type of business.

- Can reasonably be expected to achieve and maintain profitability.

- Will be operated in a safe and sound manner.

The OCC also considers a proposed bank's plans for helping to meet the credit needs of its entire community, including low- and moderate-income neighborhoods, consistent with the safe and sound operation of the bank.

Organizing Group

The organizing group must be comprised of five or more persons. Although a tribe may participate in organizing a bank, the organizers must be individuals (e.g., members of the tribe or business leaders in the community). Many, if not all, of the organizers normally serve as the bank's initial board of directors. The president of the proposed bank, who is usually the chief executive officer (CEO), must be a board member.

Generally, every national bank director must own stock of the bank and be a citizen of the United States throughout his or her term of service (12 USC 72). In addition, every director must meet residency requirements (12 USC 72); however, the OCC has discretion to waive those requirements. (See the "Director Waivers" booklet of the licensing manual.)

Importance of the CEO

Selection of a qualified CEO is one of the organizing group's most important decisions affecting the success of the new bank. Together, the organizing group and its CEO must have the experience, competence, willingness, and ability to direct the proposed bank's affairs actively in a safe, sound, and legal manner.

The OCC considers the CEO as essential for a new bank's success. The proposed CEO should:

- Be involved actively in developing the proposed bank's business plan and in implementing it successfully once the bank opens.

- Have strong leadership skills and have managed a bank or similar financial institution successfully or have successful experience as a bank officer in areas relevant to the proposed bank's marketing strategy and needs.

- Possess skills that complement those of the directors and other proposed members of the executive officer team, including extensive experience in operations or administration.

Capital Considerations

An organizing group must raise a sufficient amount of capital to pay all organization costs, compete effectively in the market area, and support planned operations adequately. The OCC's chartering policy in 12 CFR 5.20 states that a proposed bank must have capital sufficient to protect against the various risks inherent in the bank's business plan. This initial capital is net of organizing expenses that will be charted to the bank's capital after it begins operations.

An organizing group, therefore, must raise a sufficient amount of capital to pay all organization costs, compete effectively in the market area, and support planned operations adequately. Initial capitalization must also be sufficient to maintain adequate capital levels, until the bank achieves profitable operations. A new bank's business plan should identify capital adequate to address uncertainties in the marketplace and demonstrate a clear ability to raise additional capital, if needed. (See the Sources of Capital and Deposits section of this guide for a discussion of possible sources of capital.)

The OCC does not set minimum capital amounts for charter proposal differences over projected bank operations, management, and local market conditions. The initial capital plan of a new bank is reviewed against its business plan to determine if the proposed capital will be sufficient to support the projected volume and type of business proposed by the organizing group.

The OCC will require proposed banks with higher risk profiles to have higher capital reserves than those of proposed banks that present lower risk. The OCC expects projected capital for new banks to remain at or above the "well capitalized" level, as defined in 12 CFR 6.4(b)(1), for the first three years of operation. These are "minimum capital standards."

The Federal Deposit Insurance Corporation (FDIC) has requirements similar to those of the OCC for obtaining federal deposit insurance. The FDIC's statement of policy[6] requires that initial capital should be sufficient to provide a Tier 1 capital to assets leverage ratio of no less than 8 percent throughout the first three years of operation.

Stock must be subscribed from and issued to shareholders of national banks. National banks may not create classes of common stock with different or no voting rights. Federal banking law provides, without exception, that common shareholders are entitled to one vote per share held in all matters, except the election of directors. At that time, shareholders have cumulative voting rights.

---

[6] See FDIC Statement of Policy on Applications for Deposit Insurance, 63 Fed. Reg. 44,756, August 20, 1998, effective October 1, 1998. Also see www.fdic.gov/lawsregs/rules/5000-9.html.

Common stock represents ownership of the bank. There is a direct correlation between the value of the common stock and the value of the bank with dividends to common shareholders tied to the earnings of the bank. The OCC generally discourages use of preferred stock in the initial capital structure of a new national bank because it is more costly than common stock, though its use is not prohibited.

Preferred stock is more similar to a debt instrument in that it usually has a dividend rate either fixed at the time of issuance or based on a market rate of interest plus a credit spread and is not tied to the earnings of the bank. Dividends on preferred stock create a bank obligation that may prevent the bank from retaining earnings to fund future growth. Investors may be reluctant to purchase common stock of a bank with a significant amount of preferred stock.

The OCC may determine that including a significant amount of preferred stock in a bank's capital structure could lead to instability in the ownership of the bank or otherwise adversely affect the safety and soundness of the institution. Such a determination would justify disapproval of the charter application or revocation of a preliminary conditional approval already issued.

The OCC generally is opposed to debt-based capitalization of a new bank. If any debt will be issued by an affiliate to capitalize the bank, the organizing group must demonstrate that debt service requirements can be met without reliance on cash flows *of any kind* from the bank.

Community Development Banks

Prospective bank organizers may chose to charter a national bank with a community development focus (CD bank). A CD bank is a depository institution with a stated mission primarily to promote the public welfare, including the welfare of low- and moderate-income (LMI) communities or families, in which it is chartered to conduct business. A CD bank provides financial services that primarily benefit LMI persons, LMI areas, or other areas targeted for redevelopment by local, state, tribal, or federal government (including federal government enterprise communities and federal empowerment zones). CD bank applicants must meet the same statutory, regulatory, and procedural requirements as other nationally chartered banks. The OCC applies its standard charter policies and procedures that are set forth in 12 CFR 5 and the manual.

A CD bank proposal typically has two unique processing features. First, a CD bank most likely will want to receive a "CD focus" designation from the OCC, so that other national banks may invest in it under the investment authority of 12 USC 24 (Eleventh) and 12 CFR 24 as well as under 12 CFR 5.36. Although the OCC determines whether a bank charter should be granted, it also uses 12 CFR 24 criteria to decide if the CD designation request should be approved. That designation request is integrated into the chartering process.[7] Second, the OCC provides technical assistance (TA) to the organizers of a CD bank prior to the charter prefiling meeting.

The Licensing Department oversees the chartering process and serves as the primary point of contact for the entire licensing process. The department assembles for each CD bank proposal a processing team that typically includes staff from licensing, legal, and community development. The processing team works closely throughout the charter process for a CD bank. It may meet with organizers and provide information on issues and processes involved in the chartering process. (See Appendix D for additional information on chartering a CD bank.)

Acquisition by Merger

A common way to acquire a bank is to merge or consolidate it with an "interim bank" — a non-operational bank created solely to facilitate the merger or consolidation. This method of acquisition is called a business combination and often has certain tax and accounting benefits over acquiring directly the stock of an existing bank. A business combination is subject to review by the primary federal regulator of the bank that remains after the transaction is completed (resulting bank) under the Bank Merger Act (BMA). Prior to filing, the acquirer should seek advice from its accounting experts.

Use of an Interim Bank

The general procedures for establishing an "interim" bank and entering into a business combination are contained in the "Business Combinations" booklet of the licensing manual. Although the statutes for business combinations are different from those for a charter, the OCC conducts the same review it would normally do for a charter when the acquirer does not already own a bank.

An Indian tribe, alternatively, could use an interim bank to acquire the assets and assume the liabilities of branches of a bank, rather than an entire bank. In that case, the OCC reviews the operations of the target branches, instead of those of the target bank, to assess the financial and managerial resources and future prospects of the resulting institution.

---

[7]For additional guidance on 12 CFR 24 or 12 CFR 5.36 requirements for national banks with a CD focus, see the OCC memo to prospective community development banks' organizing groups dated October 3, 2001 (see Appendix D).

Bank Merger Act Processing

Under the BMA, the applicant files its application with the primary federal regulator (responsible agency) of the resulting bank. The applicant also publishes notice of the proposed transaction no less than three times during a 30-day public comment period. Upon receipt of the application, the responsible agency contacts the other federal bank regulatory agencies and the Department of Justice, which also may comment on the application during a 30-day review period. The responsible agency reviews the application and any comments it receives from the public and decides the transaction based on:

- The effect of the transaction on competition.

- The financial and managerial resources and future prospects of the combining institutions.

- The institutions' Community Reinvestment Act (CRA) records of performance in helping to meet the credit needs of the relevant communities. (See the Community Reinvestment Act section in this guide.)

- The effect of the transaction on the convenience and needs of the community to be served and whether products and services will be reduced, including the closing of bank offices, following the transaction. The "convenience and needs" factor can be distinguished from the CRA factor in that the convenience and needs analysis is prospective, whereas the CRA factor requires the OCC to consider the applicants' records of past performance.

Acquiring the Stock of an Existing Bank

Parties who wish to acquire control of a national bank by obtaining its voting stock, rather than by chartering a new bank, must notify the OCC and submit certain information described in the "Change in Bank Control" booklet of the licensing manual.

Notification is required by any person acquiring 25 percent or more of a class of voting securities of a national bank. If no one owns 25 percent of more of a class of voting securities, notification also is required by persons acquiring 10 percent to 25 percent. Such persons are presumed to have acquired control unless this presumption is rebutted successfully. The percentage ownership thresholds can be reached by combining shares of persons acting in concert.

The OCC must receive the notice at least 60 days prior to the acquisition. Although the OCC may extend the review period for up to 120 more days, it normally completes its review, including background investigations, during the initial 60-day review period. The notice is subject to a public notice and comment period.

Decision Criteria

The Change in Bank Control Act (CBCA) establishes the criteria for deciding whether to disapprove the notice. The OCC may disapprove a change in control if it finds that:

- The proposed acquisition of control would result in a monopoly or would further any monopoly or an attempt to monopolize the business of banking anywhere in the United States.

- The effect of the proposed acquisition may lessen competition substantially, tend to create a monopoly, or in any other manner restrain trade, and the anticompetitive effects are not outweighed clearly by benefits to the convenience and needs of the community to be served.

- The financial condition of any acquiring party might jeopardize the stability of the bank or prejudice the interests of the depositors.

- The competence, experience, or integrity of any of the acquiring party(ies) or of the proposed management indicate that it would not be in the interests of the depositors and the public for such persons to control the bank.

- The acquirer does not provide the OCC with all required information.

- The proposal would result in an adverse effect on the deposit insurance funds.

Tribes Acquiring Bank Stock

The officials of a tribal entity, such as a business committee or tribal council, that acquire national bank stock must comply with the CBCA notice and background information requirements. When a tribal official who participates in voting the bank's stock is replaced by election, appointment, or otherwise, the OCC requires the new official to provide the prior notice and background information before he or she can participate in the affairs of the bank.

Use of a Voting Trust or Agreement

Because of routine changes in tribal officials through elections, tribes could face continuing CBCA notice requirements. To reduce CBCA filing burden, some tribes have transferred voting control of the bank stock away from elected officials through a voting trust or agreement. For example, a tribe may establish a voting trust, in which the trustee will serve for a long period of time and may not be replaced by the tribe without cause. As long as the voting trust provides absolute voting control to such a trustee, the OCC would apply the CBCA requirements to the trustee, and not to the tribal officials who face regular elections.[8]

Alternatively, voting control also can be transferred through a voting agreement in which the tribe agrees to vote the bank stock according to the direction of someone not subject to regular replacement. For example, the tribe can agree to vote its stock in the same proportional manner as other stockholders. For as long as this voting agreement is in place, changes in tribal officials will not trigger the prior notice requirements of the CBCA. The "Change in Bank Control" booklet of the licensing manual provides greater detail on voting trusts and agreements.

Use of a Bank Holding Company

A tribe that charters or acquires control of a national bank may consider holding the bank stock either directly or through a subordinate entity. If the tribe holds the stock through a subordinate entity, such as a corporation, that entity could be considered to be a bank holding company subject to regulation and examination by the FRB. A tribe proposing to own a national bank through a bank holding company would have to apply to the FRB for approval to organize the holding company.

A bank holding company and its affiliates can engage only in activities closely related to banking. Therefore, the bank holding company could not hold or own certain governmental or commercial activities (e.g., a hospital or gaming enterprise).

On several occasions, the FRB has determined that a tribe would not be considered a bank holding company.[9] Accordingly, a tribe that owns

---

[8]Tribes considering using a voting trust should consult with legal counsel or the appropriate Federal Reserve Bank regarding whether the voting trust would be considered a bank holding company subject to supervision and regulation under the Bank Holding Company Act.

[9]See Chickasaw Banc Holding Company, 88 Federal Reserve Bulletin 229 (2002); Native American Bancorporation Co., 87 Federal Reserve Bulletin 747 (2001); Mille Lacs Bancorporation, Inc., 82 Federal Reserve Bulletin 336 (1996); Bay Bancorporation, 81 Federal Reserve Bulletin 791 (1995).

nonbanking activities outside of a bank holding company would not be required to divest those activities if it acquired a bank. In reaching this conclusion, the FRB relied on the status of a tribe as a sovereign nation — and not a company — under federal law.

The FRB also relied on several commitments made by the tribes. Those commitments were designed to:

- Ensure that the FRB had sufficient access to information from the tribes and their affiliates to determine compliance with federal banking laws.

- Address potential safety and soundness concerns that could arise if a tribe operates diverse nonbanking ventures (e.g., gaming facilities).

The OCC has required similar commitments in previous cases. An example of language used to ensure examiner access to information and the ability of the federal banking regulators to bring administrative actions appears in a Sample Commitment Letter in Appendix B. Appendix C explains the commitments. (See also the Sovereign Immunity section of this guide.)

The FRB and the OCC also have relied upon similar commitments made by tribes that collectively own a national bank in which no one tribe individually controls the bank or its parent bank holding company.[10]

Conversion

Another alternative for entering the national banking system is to convert an institution with a different type of charter. Under applicable statutes and regulations, state banks, state savings banks, and other state banking institutions engaged in the business of receiving deposits, as well as federal savings associations, may be converted directly to national bank charters.[11] The conversion can occur either before or after the tribe acquires the bank. Conversions generally are not subject to a public notice and comment period. In determining action on a conversion application, the OCC normally considers the institution's:

- Condition and management, including compliance with regulatory capital requirements.

- Conformance with statutory criteria, including many of the same

---

[10]Native American Bancorporation Co., 87 Federal Reserve Bulletin 747 (2001) and OCC Interpretative Letter #493 (September 28, 2001).

[11]Indirect conversions also could occur through merging an interim national bank with the state-chartered entity or federal savings association. For a discussion of the use of interim banks to enter the national banking system, see the previous section on Acquisition by Merger.

---

standards applicable to chartering a new national bank.

- Adequacy of policies, practices, and procedures that parallel the OCC's "Minimum Policies and Procedures." (See the Appendix of the "Charters" booklet of the licensing manual for specific information.)

- CRA record of performance.

The OCC may deny a conversion application for any of the reasons listed under the Decisions section appearing later in this guide. In addition, the OCC may deny an application if the applicant attempts to use it to escape supervisory action by the current regulator. A detailed discussion of conversion transactions is contained in the "Conversions" booklet of the licensing manual.

The OCC acts on applications to establish or acquire national banks and on filings for mergers, branches, and other structural changes in accordance with the requirements in national banking laws and OCC regulations.

Prefiling Discussions and Meetings

Before filing an application, the organizers or investors must appoint a spokesperson to contact the OCC's Licensing staff in the district office that serves the area in which the bank will be located to discuss corporate proposals. (See Appendix F.) The spokesperson, serves as the primary liaison between the OCC and the group of organizers or investors. Prefiling communications may take the form of formal prefiling meetings or more informal discussions or conference calls.

During this exploratory or prefiling period, the OCC provides technical assistance to tribes interested in seeking entry into the national banking system. This advisory role may include a one-time prefiling review of draft applications, but does not extend to preparation of applications.

The OCC requires all independent groups seeking to charter a *de novo* bank to participate in a prefiling meeting with OCC staff. Accordingly, when the group is ready to proceed with filing an application, the group's spokesperson contacts the OCC's Licensing staff to schedule a prefiling meeting. Prior to the meeting, the organizers should review appropriate materials to become familiar with the policies and procedures associated with the charter process. The OCC expects all organizers of the proposed new national bank to attend the prefiling meeting.

At the prefiling meeting, or in informal discussions, the Licensing staff reviews with the organizing group the OCC's chartering policy and procedures, supervisory perspectives that may affect the proposal specifically, and the requirements for filing a charter application and organizing a national bank. (See the "Charters" booklet of the licensing manual.)

For other types of filings, an applicant may request a prefiling meeting with OCC staff to review a proposed transaction and the applicable processing steps, or the OCC may require a prefiling meeting. Regardless of the type of application, when requested, OCC staff will conduct the prefiling meeting at a location proposed by the filer rather than at the OCC.

Filing the Application

After completion of the prefiling phase, the group files its corporate application with the Licensing staff in the district office that serves the area in which the bank will be located. The OCC expects each filer to prepare accurately and completely each filing submitted to it. Each applicant certifies that neither its filing nor any supporting materials contain misrepresentations or omissions.

In addition, each filer should:

- Submit all necessary information about a proposed corporate filing to aid the OCC in reaching an informed decision quickly.

- Determine compliance with all applicable statutes and regulations.

- Seek advice, as appropriate, from banking and tribal attorneys.

The OCC provides more detailed information about filing each type of corporate application in other booklets of the licensing manual. Those booklets also outline the related policies and procedures for each type of application.

Filing Fees

The OCC publishes a corporate filing fee schedule at least annually in a bulletin entitled, "Notice of Comptroller of the Currency Fees." The OCC mails the bulletin to all national banks. A copy of the current bulletin may be obtained from the OCC's Communications Division by calling (202) 874-4700 or by visiting the OCC's Web site at http://www.occ.treas.gov.

The appropriate filing fee, payable by check or other means to the "Comptroller of the Currency," should accompany the application.

Fee Waivers

The OCC generally does not refund filing fees. However, when justified by the OCC's processing cost or in extenuating circumstances, the OCC may grant a request for a fee waiver, reduction, or refund (fee concession). In some cases, the OCC will reduce its fees to account for special circumstances or reduced processing requirements. For example, the OCC has reduced its CBCA processing fees for newly elected or appointed tribal officials who will exercise control over bank stock after the initial CBCA notice. Those fees are reduced because the review typically is limited to the new official(s) and does not cover the entire tribal council or business committee.

The filer may request a fee concession in writing, with justification, to the licensing manager in the appropriate district office before or simultaneously with submission of its corporate filing. The OCC decides all requests individually.

New Charters in Low- or Moderate-Income Areas

The OCC does not require a corporate filing fee for the charter of a new bank that will be located in an area that meets the following two requirements:

- The area is a low- or moderate-income area as defined by 12 CFR 25.12(l), (n)(1), and (n)(2), which could include an Indian reservation.

- No other depository institution operates a branch or main office in that area.

Background Investigations

The OCC requires each proposed organizer, director, principal shareholder, and executive officer to submit biographical and financial reports in connection with applications for *de novo* charters and certain other types of corporate applications. The OCC conducts background checks to assess a person's competence, experience, integrity, and/or financial ability. The OCC will determine independently the accuracy and completeness of the information submitted for each person and must be satisfied that each person is qualified to serve in the proposed capacity. (See the *Interagency Biographical and Financial Reports form in the* "Background Investigations" booklet of the licensing manual.)

Decisions

The OCC evaluates the entire filing to determine whether the applicant may complete the transaction legally and operate the proposed activity in a safe and sound manner. Each filing is evaluated on its merits.

The OCC may approve or conditionally approve any filing after reviewing the application and considering the relevant factors. The OCC may impose conditions if it determines that they are necessary or appropriate to ensure that approval is consistent with applicable statutes, regulations, and OCC policies.

The OCC may deny a filing for reasons, including:

- The existence of significant supervisory, CRA (if applicable), or compliance concerns.

- Approval would be inconsistent with applicable law or regulations and OCC policy.

- The applicant fails to provide in a timely manner information that the OCC requested to make an informed decision.

Time Considerations

While the OCC has established standard processing times, many applications from tribes present special issues. Accordingly, processing times for such applications may exceed the standard time estimates.

Supervision of National Banks

The OCC supervises national banks through onsite examinations and off-site monitoring. (See the "Large Bank Supervision" and "Community Bank Supervision" booklets of the *Comptroller's Handbook*.) Those activities help ascertain the condition of individual banks and the overall stability of the national banking system. The OCC determines the frequency of its onsite examinations (the supervisory cycle) based on the bank's size, complexity, risk profile, and condition. Onsite examinations normally are conducted either annually or up to every 18 months (12 CFR 4.6).

Examiners meet with bank management during the examination to obtain information or discuss issues. When the examination is complete, the examiners prepare a report and conduct a meeting with the bank's board of directors to discuss the results. Directors review and sign the report of examination.

An environment in which examiners and board members openly and honestly communicate benefits a bank. OCC examiners and professional staff have experience with a broad range of banking activities and can provide independent, objective information on safe and sound banking principles and compliance with laws and regulations.

Board of Directors' Oversight

A national bank, as other corporate organizations, has shareholders who elect a board of directors. A bank's board of directors oversees the management of the bank's activities. Directors must exercise reasonable care when guiding the bank's affairs.

Bank directors face unique challenges because banks differ from other corporations. Although banks, as other corporations, use their capital to support their activities, most of the funds banks put at risk belong to others, primarily depositors. Banks lend and invest customers' deposits to earn a profit and a reasonable return to shareholders and to meet the credit needs of the community. Properly managing risk to serve those interests is a critical challenge faced by the board and bank management.

As corporate board members, banks' directors have duties to the banking corporations they serve. Those duties are known as the duties of diligence and loyalty.

The duty of diligence means that directors must devote the time and attention necessary to enhance safe, sound, and legal operations of the bank. Directors must attend directors' meetings, review meeting materials, and ask questions and seek explanations to understand the issues completely. They must use independent judgment and be objective when overseeing the bank's affairs. The director's decision-making process should involve careful consideration of reasonably available and relevant information.

The duty of loyalty means that directors must never put their own interests above those of the bank they serve. The duty of loyalty requires directors to administer the affairs of the bank with candor, personal honesty, and integrity. Relationships with the bank must always be at arms-length. In addition, directors may not take business opportunities away from the bank inappropriately.

Directors and national banks are accountable, not only to their shareholders and depositors, but also to their regulators. The risks inherent in banking, the safety net provided by deposit insurance, and the importance of a safe and sound banking system to the nation's economy make this oversight appropriate.

The long-term health of a bank depends on a strong, independent, and attentive board. Although a board of directors does not guarantee the bank's success, it must oversee bank operations to ensure that the bank conducts business in a safe and sound manner. The board must keep informed about the bank's operating environment; hire and retain competent management; and ensure that the bank has a risk management structure and process suitable for the bank's size and activities. The board also must oversee the bank's business performance and ensure that the bank serves the community's credit needs. Problems arising from failures in any of those areas represent the board's failure to exercise properly its oversight responsibilities and can result in individual liability if a director has not acted as a reasonably prudent director would act in similar circumstances.

More information about the role of a bank director is available in the OCC's *The Director's Book: The Role of the National Bank Director* (*The Director's Book*). (See Appendix G for information about how to acquire this publication.)

Enforcement Actions

The OCC, in the furtherance of its duty to supervise national banks, can respond in several ways to violations of laws, rules, or regulations or unsafe or unsound practices or conditions. Upon discovery of serious safety and soundness or compliance problems, the OCC will take corrective and remedial action. The "report of examination" identifies and communicates clearly the OCC's assessment of a bank's condition and describes its problems, areas of concern or weaknesses, and the primary cause of each. Once those problems have been communicated to a bank, its senior management and board of directors will be expected to take appropriate corrective measures. Those actions will be important in determining whether and what enforcement action the OCC should take.

The OCC may take enforcement actions against the bank or against parties affiliated with banks. Most commonly, the OCC's enforcement actions are brought against banks and their officers and directors. Actions against shareholders are rare, unless the shareholders otherwise are involved directly in bank management or in an illegal, unsafe or unsound activity with the bank. Enforcement actions may be informal or formal. (See *The Director's Book* for a more complete discussion of enforcement actions available to the OCC.)

Sovereign Immunity

Under the federal-tribal relationship described previously in the Tribal Sovereignty section of this guide, Indian tribes retain their original sovereign powers, unless divested of those powers by the United States.[12] Thus, Indian tribes possess sovereign immunity from lawsuits by states or private citizens in the absence of a tribal government waiver or congressional abrogation of tribal sovereign immunity.[13] Indian tribes are "dependent" on the federal government, so tribal sovereign immunity does not bar suit by the United States against a tribe to enforce federal law.[14]

The OCC must be able to examine a national bank and its affiliates expeditiously to determine the legality and safety and soundness of transactions between them. Because of the nature of bank regulation and supervision, any delay in the OCC supervisory process resulting from a claim of sovereign immunity may interfere with the supervision of the bank and could hamper the OCC's ability to use enforcement actions to deter unsafe or unsound banking practices. Accordingly, the OCC and other federal banking regulators have taken the position that tribes proposing to establish or acquire a bank must agree not to raise a claim of tribal sovereign immunity as a defense to any regulatory or enforcement action in any administrative or

---

[12]Merrion v. Jicarilla Apache Tribe, 455 U.S. 130 (1982).

[13]Kiowa Tribe v. Manufacturing Technologies, 118 S.Ct. 1700 (1998); Oklahoma Tax Comm'n v. Potawatomi Indian Tribe of Oklahoma, 498 U.S. 505 (1991); Santa Clara Pueblo v. Martinez, 436 U.S. 49 (1978); Puyallup Tribe v. Department of Game, 433 U.S. 165 (1977); United States v. U.S. Fidelity & Guaranty Co., 309 U.S. 506 (1940).

[14]Similarly, state sovereign immunity does not bar suit by the federal government against a state.

judicial forum. (See Appendixes B and C.)

In meetings with OCC staff, tribal officials have expressed interest in:

- Permissible banking activities.

- Safety and soundness protections.

- Sources of capital and deposits.

- Branching.

- Compliance issues.

Permissible Banking Activities

Bank Powers

National banks are formed under, and derive their powers from, federal law. The National Bank Act lists specific activities in which national banks may engage. National banks may also engage in "all such incidental powers as shall be necessary to carry on the business of banking" (12 USC 24 (Seventh)). The OCC and the courts base many of the activities performed by national banks on interpretations of this language over the years. Since those interpretations are evolving constantly, it is impossible to provide a complete list of all the activities that are permissible for national banks. However, some of the more common activities include:

- Accepting deposits.

- Making secured and unsecured loans for both personal and business purposes.

- Making real estate loans.

- Issuing credit cards.

- Providing safe deposit and fiduciary services.

- Selling or investing in government (including state, local, and tribal) bonds.

- Selling or investing in permissible securities.

- Selling insurance and annuities.

The OCC's legal staff in the districts and in Washington can provide more information about specific activities in which tribes may be interested. (See Appendix F for a list of contacts, the "Investment in Subsidiaries and Equity" booklet of the licensing manual, and "Activities Permissible for A National Bank" on the OCC's Web site for more information.)

Community Development Opportunities

Federal law also encourages national banks to engage in CD lending and investment activities, which may be of particular interest to tribally owned banks. Banks can use these activities to:

- Increase market penetration.

- Help businesses, organizations, and persons make transitions into more traditional banking relationships.

- Supplement the bank's regular loans and investments.

In addition, banks may receive positive consideration during their CRA evaluations for CD loans and investments if they meet the criteria under the CRA regulations.

Banks deliver CD financial services in a variety of ways. A bank must consider carefully its resources and its goals when determining which organizational mechanisms to use to facilitate its CD financing.

Lending Consortia

Perhaps the most significant trend in bank CD finance has been the extraordinary growth in the number and scope of multibank consortia. In large and small communities throughout the country, banks and other financial institutions are joining with public and private entities to form intermediary organizations focused on one or more community development objectives.

Lender consortia have been formed for a variety of purposes. In addition to their own programs, banks often participate in one or more consortium arrangements that provide financing for low- and moderate-income housing, small business development, downtown and neighborhood commercial revitalization, or industrial expansion.

Multibank consortia may be formal or informal. Their forms depend on their purpose and the extent to which other community resources and participants are available. The primary forms of multibank consortia include loan pools and multibank lending corporations.

Public Welfare Investments

In addition to their other investment authority, national banks may make investments designed primarily to promote the public welfare, including that of LMI communities or families (such as by providing housing, services, or jobs). A national bank may make such investments directly or by purchasing interests in an entity primarily engaged in making such investments. (12 USC 24 (Eleventh).) Under 12 CFR 24, national banks may make CD investments in entities that serve the public welfare.

Using this authority, national banks may invest in community development corporations (CDCs) and community development projects (CD projects). Those investments must primarily benefit LMI persons, LMI areas, or other areas targeted for redevelopment by local, state, tribal, or federal government (including federal enterprise communities and federal empowerment zones) (12 CFR 24). For example, national banks have created or invested in CDCs and CD projects that:

- Acquire, rehabilitate, construct, manage, market, and sell housing, commercial, and industrial projects.

- Make equity investments in small businesses.

- Participate as limited partners in joint ventures related to community development.

- Provide or arrange additional debt financing for projects in which the CDC is involved.

A national bank may invest up to five percent or, with prior OCC approval, up to 10 percent of its capital and surplus in investments designed primarily to promote the public welfare.

Some national banks have established for-profit and/or nonprofit CDCs. Other national banks have invested in multibank or other multi-investor CDCs, existing neighborhood CDCs, limited partnerships for affordable housing, or consortium corporations, the activities of which meet the statutory and regulatory requirements. Multibank and multi-investor CDCs often are developed for larger, more complex CD projects.

Small Business Investment Companies

National banks may also invest in small business investment companies (SBICs) (15 USC 682(b)). SBICs are venture capital firms licensed by the U.S. Small Business Administration. Typically, SBICs support small business expansion through a combination of longer-term debt, equity investments, and management counseling. SBICs also have certain tax advantages not available to banks.

A SBIC can be organized in any state as either a corporation or a limited partnership. Most SBICs are owned by relatively small groups of local investors. However, some SBICs are corporations with publicly traded stock, and some are subsidiaries of corporations, including banks and bank holding companies.

Bank ownership of a SBIC subsidiary permits banks to invest indirectly in small businesses in which they could not have invested otherwise, because of banking laws and regulations. In addition to the public welfare investment limits described earlier, a bank may invest up to five percent of its capital and surplus in SBICs.

Other Types of CD Opportunities

National banks can explore several other types of CD lending and investing opportunities. Banks may purchase securities backed by interests in pools of CD loans (e.g., loans for affordable housing or small businesses). Banks also can purchase certain municipal or mortgage revenue bonds issued by state, municipal, and tribal authorities. Banks must conduct those activities consistent with the requirements and limitations of 12 USC 24 (Seventh) and the OCC's implementing regulation (12 CFR 1). National banks should contact OCC's Community Development Division at (202) 874-4930 for more information about those programs and OCC's Bank Activities and Structure Division at (202) 874-5300 for information about legal requirements.

Fiduciary Activities

Federal banking law authorizes national banks to engage in fiduciary activities (12 USC 92a). Examples of fiduciary activities include acting as trustee, executor, administrator, transfer agent, custodian under a uniform gifts to minors act, investment advisor (if the bank receives a fee for its investment advice), or any capacity in which the bank possesses investment discretion on behalf of another (12 CFR 9.2).

National banks may offer fiduciary services to their customers upon receipt of OCC approval for such activities (12 CFR 5.26). (See the "Fiduciary Powers" booklet of the licensing manual.) The OCC generally permits a national bank to exercise fiduciary powers if it is operating in a satisfactory manner, the proposed activities comply with relevant statutes and regulations, and the bank retains qualified fiduciary management (12 CFR 9). National banks located in Indian country should consult with bank counsel to determine whether applicable law, as defined by 12 CFR 9.2 (b), permits specific fiduciary activities and investments.

National banks interested in conducting fiduciary activities should contact the appropriate district office (see Appendix F) or the Licensing Department at (202) 874-5060.

Safety and Soundness Protections

Federal banking law includes certain restrictions on the business of banking to ensure the safety and soundness of the national banking system. For example, federal law limits:

- Transactions between a bank and its "affiliates."

- Loans to "insiders."

- Direct bank involvement in gaming or lottery activities.

Affiliate Transactions

Sections 23A and 23B of the Federal Reserve Act (FRA)[15] are designed to protect a bank from loss in transactions with its affiliates. Section 23A defines "affiliate" to include, among other things, any "company" that controls a bank and any company that is under common control with the bank. Subsidiaries of banks generally are not considered to be affiliates of the bank.

Section 23A of the FRA

Section 23A protects banks by:

- Limiting "covered transactions" with any single affiliate to no more than 10 percent of the bank's capital and surplus, and aggregate transactions with all affiliates to no more than 20 percent of capital and surplus. Covered transactions include:

  — A bank's extensions of credit to, or guarantees on behalf of, its affiliates or purchases of assets from its affiliates.

---

[15]12 USC 371c and 371c-1.

— Investments in securities issued by affiliates.

— Other specified transactions exposing the bank to risk of abuse by its affiliates.

- Requiring that all transactions between a bank and its affiliates be made on terms consistent with safe and sound banking practices. In particular, a bank may not purchase low-quality assets from the bank's affiliates.

- Requiring that all guarantees and extensions of credit to an affiliate be secured by a statutorily defined amount of collateral.[16]

Section 23B of the FRA

Section 23B requires a bank to engage in transactions with its nonbank affiliates only on terms and under circumstances that are substantially the same or at least as favorable to the bank as those prevailing at the time for comparable transactions with unaffiliated companies. This requirement generally means that transactions with nonbank affiliates must be conducted on an arm's-length basis. Thus, for example, pricing must reflect fair market value. Section 23B applies this restriction to any covered transaction, as defined by section 23A, and to other specified transactions, such as a sale of securities/assets and the payment of money or the furnishing of services to a nonbank affiliate.

Status of Tribes and Tribal Subunits as "Affiliates"

In considering the application of sections 23A and 23B to a tribally controlled bank, one must identify entities that are bank "affiliates." Because Indian tribes and their political/governmental subdivisions enjoy a unique legal status, the FRB has determined that they are not "companies" for purposes of the BHCA. Therefore, a tribe's status as an "affiliate" of the bank for purposes of sections 23A and 23B is unclear. Both the FRB and the OCC, however, routinely require tribes seeking to organize or acquire banks to commit that all tribal entities will be deemed to be "affiliates" of the bank for purposes of sections 23A and 23B. (See Appendixes B and C.)

A tribal bank's covered transactions with its affiliates (e.g., the tribe's housing authority, library, hospital, gaming enterprise, hotel, restaurant, or construction or agricultural company) will be subject to the restrictions of sections 23A and 23B. As a result, the bank's guarantees on behalf of, and loans to those entities, are subject to section 23A's quantitative limits and

---

[16]A full or partial exemption from these restrictions may be available for certain statutorily prescribed types of transactions. See, for example, section 23A(d).

collateralization requirements. Similarly, if a tribal bank wishes to purchase loans or other assets from the tribe or a tribal entity, it must comply with:

- Section 23A's quantitative limits.

- Section 23A's prohibition against banks purchasing low-quality assets from affiliates.

- Section 23B's requirement that assets be purchased at fair market value.

Asset purchases need not be collateralized, however.

Loans to "Insiders"

The OCC and the FRB require a tribe and all of its subunits and businesses to agree to be treated as insiders of its tribally owned bank for purposes of the FRB's Regulation O (12 CFR 215) and the OCC's part 31 (12 CFR 31). This means that the bank must comply with the quantitative and qualitative limits of those regulations whenever it makes a loan or extension of credit to the tribe or its subunits or businesses, as well as when the bank lends to its insiders (i.e., officers, directors, and controlling shareholders and their related interests).

Under those regulations, a bank (subject to a number of regulatory and statutory exceptions) may not make a loan to an insider in an amount that exceeds 15 percent of the bank's capital and surplus. In addition, a bank cannot extend preferential loans to insiders. Additional restrictions and requirements apply to loans to executive officers and other types of insider loans under those regulations.

Gaming

A tribe may own a national bank even if it also operates a gaming operation. However, several legal restrictions prevent direct involvement in lottery or gaming activity by national banks. For instance, national banks are forbidden from selling or redeeming lottery tickets or gambling chips, or permitting others to do so on their banking premises. In addition, direct public access from the bank to a casino is prohibited (12 USC 25a). However, a national bank can provide routine banking services to a casino or gaming enterprise, subject to the restrictions on transactions with affiliates and insiders as described previously. Further, a national bank can operate an Automated Teller Machine (ATM) on casino premises.

Sources of Capital and Deposits

Most new banks, and many new bank holding companies, raise capital by selling common stock to the public. The OCC has no general prohibition against the inclusion of preferred stock in the initial capital structure of a new national bank. However, the OCC may determine that the inclusion of a significant amount of preferred stock in a bank's capital structure could lead to instability in the ownership of the bank or otherwise adversely affect the safety and soundness of the institution. Such a determination would justify disapproval of the charter application or revocation of a preliminary approval already issued.

Capital from Financial Institutions

As described in the New National Bank Charter section of this guide, when the OCC grants preliminary approval to a charter with a community development focus, federally insured financial institutions may make equity investments in a CD bank as a CD project.[17] These investor banks may receive positive consideration under CRA for their investment. In addition to having an ownership stake in the institution, banks may serve as advisors; lend staff, including senior and executive management; contribute facilities, equipment, and expertise; and sit as directors, along with community leaders, on their governing boards.

CDFI Fund

The Community Development Banking and Financial Institutions Act established the Community Development Financial Institutions (CDFI) Fund (CDFI Fund) as a wholly owned government corporation. The CDFI Fund's responsibility is to facilitate the flow of capital and services to underserved communities and persons that have been unable to take advantage of traditional financial thoroughfares. It accomplishes this through the administration of funding and technical assistance programs, briefly described as follows. Additional information about these programs, including applications, is available by visiting the CDFI Fund's Web site at http://www.cdfifund.gov or by phoning (202) 622-8662.

CDFI Core Component

The Core Component is the CDFI Fund's main program under which CDFIs, or entities proposing to become CDFIs, may apply for financial and technical assistance. National banks with a community development focus may apply

---

[17]However, any one national bank proposing to invest in a CD bank must limit its investment to avoid being considered a bank holding company under the Bank Holding Company Act.

for equity capital and technical assistance from the CDFI Fund. The investments of the CDFI program are intended to provide much-needed capital to those institutions.

Under the CDFI program, the fund provides assistance to selected applicants to enhance their ability to make loans and investments and provide services to benefit designated investment area(s) or, targeted population(s), or both (12 CFR 1805.200). The statute specifically recognizes that Indian tribes may be targeted populations (12 USC 4702 (20)). The fund selects eligible awardees through a competitive application process.

BEA Program Component

Another program administered by the CDFI Fund is the Bank Enterprise Act (BEA) Program. The BEA program is intended to encourage insured depository institutions to increase loans, services, and technical assistance within distressed communities and to make equity investments in CDFIs. The BEA program rewards participating insured depository institutions for increasing their activities in economically distressed communities and investing in CDFIs through an awards program. The selection of awardees is made through a competitive process, and awards are made only after successful completion of the specified activities.

Native American CDFI Technical Assistance (NACTA) Component

For greater access to capital on tribal lands, the CDFI Fund established a fund to provide technical assistance and training for Native American communities. The fund is intended to: increase access to capital in urban and rural Native American communities; create new CDFIs that serve these communities; and increase the capacity of existing CDFIs that currently serve Indian country. Awards are made through a competitive application process.

New Markets Tax Credit

Individual and corporate investors can make an equity investment in an eligible "community development entity" (CDE)[18] and receive a New Markets Tax Credit worth more than 30 percent of the amount invested over the life of the credit, in present value terms. Eligible CDEs could include for-profit CDFIs, for-profit subsidiaries of CDCs, SBA-licensed new markets venture capital companies,[19] and specialized small business investment companies.[20]

---

[18] See definition of CDE at 66 Fed. Reg. 21,846 (May 1, 2001).

[19] See 13 CFR part 108 for a definition of new markets venture capital company.

[20] See 13 CFR 107.50 ("Section 301(d) Licensee") for a definition of specialized small business investment company.

Tribal Funds as Deposits

Tribal funds may be a significant source of deposits for a tribally owned bank. Deposit insurance can provide some protection for the funds. Another alternative is for the depository bank to collateralize the tribal deposits with government securities owned by the bank. In fact, a bond or other collateral must secure tribal trust funds (25 USC 151, 162a). Under the National Bank Act, national banks may secure any funds deposited by a federally recognized Indian tribe by government securities prescribed by the Secretary of the Treasury (12 USC 90). Collateralized deposits that exceed the federal deposit insurance limits would have priority over non-collateralized deposits in the event of bank failure. In establishing the interest rates and other terms of those deposits from affiliated tribal entities, the bank should consider the applicability of section 23B of the Federal Reserve Act (FRA) and its restrictions on preferential contracts between affiliates. (See the previous discussion in the section on Section 23B of the FRA.)

Minority Banks

The OCC's "Policy Statement on Minority-Owned National Banks" (see Appendix E) recognizes the importance of minority-owned banks in addressing financial services needs in the minority and low-income communities they serve. It also affirms the OCC's commitment to encouraging the success of these banks through the OCC advice and technical assistance to minority bank applicants interested in entering the national banking system.

Operating minority-owned national banks also will be provided with supervisory support through regular communication and examination continuity. Additionally, the OCC maintains a list of minority-owned national banks on National Banknet to promote a dialogue with peer banks and potential investors and the use of the Comparative Analysis Reporting system that helps the bank identify its relative strengths and weaknesses. Tribally owned national banks qualify as minority-owned national banks.

Minority and women-owned banks, including tribally owned banks, may benefit from special programs. One program is the Minority Bank Deposit Program (MBDP), coordinated by the Financial Management Service (FMS) of the Department of Treasury. This federal government initiative fosters the establishment, preservation, and strengthening of minority business enterprise. It is a voluntary program to encourage federal agencies, state and local governments, and the private sector to use MBDP participants as depositaries and financial agents. Potential deposits include:

- Agency deposits of public money.

- Cash advances to federal contractors and grantees.

- Certain independent deposits (e.g., postal service deposits and certificates of deposit, certain Department of Agriculture funds and funds that the Bureau of Indian Affairs invests on behalf of Indian tribes and Alaskan native villages).

An eligible financial institution must apply to become a participant in the MBDP and receive certification from the FMS. (See Appendix H.) Additional information about the MBDP can be found online at http://www.fms.treas. gov/mbdp.

In addition to participation in the MBDP, minority and women-owned institutions may benefit from their status because the CRA encourages other banks and thrifts to engage in certain other activities with minority and women-owned institutions.[21] Those activities include:

- Donating, selling, or renting a branch location to a minority or women-owned depository institution at below market terms.

- Undertaking capital investments, loan participation, and other ventures in cooperation with minority or women-owned depository institutions, provided that those activities help meet the credit needs of local communities in which such institutions are chartered.

In addition, the OCC and other bank and thrift regulators have given as an example of a qualified investment for CRA purposes, an investment, grant, deposit or share in or to a minority- or women-owned financial institution that primarily lend or facilitate lending in low- and moderate-income areas or to low- and moderate-income individuals in order to promote community development.[22] If the minority-owned national bank's activities will not directly benefit the investor bank's CRA assessment area, the investor bank may still receive CRA consideration for an investment in the minority-owned bank if the investor bank has adequately addressed the needs of its assessment area and the activities of the minority-owned national bank benefit areas or individuals located somewhere within a broader statewide or regional area that includes the investor bank's assessment area(s).[23]

---

[21] 12 USC 2903(b) and 2907.

[22] Federal Financial Institutions Examination Council, "Community Reinvestment Act; Interagency Questions and Answers Regarding Community Reinvestment," 66 Fed. Reg. 36,620, 36,629 (July 12, 2001) (§§ __.12(s) & 563e.12(r) – 4) (hereinafter "Interagency Questions and Answers").
[23] Interagency Questions and Answers, 66 Fed. Reg. at 36,626-27 (§§ __.12(i) & 563e.12(h) – 5).

Branching

National banks, upon formation, must have a main office for the conduct of business with the public. However, they are not limited to conducting their business only from that location. A consideration for many tribes is increasing the accessibility of banking services to their members, who may have to travel great distances to do their banking. Establishing branches or alternatives to branches, such as ATMs and banking by telephone or computer, may help tribally owned national banks better serve their customers. Some national banks operating in Indian country have established mobile branches to reach remote areas of Indian reservations. The OCC will consider innovative proposals that would make banking more accessible in Indian communities.

Federal Law

If a national bank seeks to establish or acquire one or more branches to receive deposits, pay withdrawals, or make loans to customers in person, it must obtain approval from the OCC, which applies standards established in federal law. Those standards, in turn, are based on standards set forth in state law (12 USC 36).

For branching on Indian reservations, the OCC, applying federal law, historically has looked to the branching statutes of the state in which the Indian reservation is located to determine the authority of a bank to branch on an Indian reservation. The branching standards applied by the OCC under federal law vary depending on whether the branch to be established or acquired is located in the same state as the main office or other branches of the national bank.

Intrastate Branching

Federal law provides that a national bank has the same rights to branch in a state in which it is located as the state gives to a bank that it chartered. For example, if a state bank may branch anywhere and establish or acquire an unlimited number of branches within that state, a national bank would have the same expansive rights. If a state places branching limitations on a bank that it charters (e.g., to have only two branches or to have branches only within 25 miles of the main office), a national bank located in that state also would be subject to those branching limitations.

Interstate Branching

If a national bank with its main office in a particular state or territory seeks to branch in a different state (i.e., interstate branching), it can be accomplished by:

- Establishing a new branch.

- Acquiring an existing bank.

- Acquiring an existing branch from an existing bank.

Most states have some restrictions on interstate branching. Federal law applies different standards to each situation. (See the "Branches and Relocations" and "Business Combinations" booklets of the licensing manual for detailed discussions about establishing and acquiring branches.)

Mobile Branches

A mobile branch is a staffed facility, such as a van or trailer operated by a national bank that travels to various locations to transact business with bank customers that normally might be conducted at a more traditional brick and mortar branch. Those activities can include accepting deposits, paying withdrawals, and disbursing loan proceeds.

Generally, mobile branches can operate in two ways. First, they may stop at public places and provide branching services to any customer or prospective customer who stops at the facility. This type of facility may offer additional services, such as the opening of deposit and loan accounts. Alternatively, a mobile branch may operate as a messenger service that travels to the location of specific customers (e.g., a customer's home or office) to pick up deposits or pay withdrawals. In both situations, because the facility is a branch, it is subject to the provisions governing national bank branching that are discussed previously, including the requirement for OCC approval.

In addition, some national banks hire a third party messenger service to pick up deposits and pay withdrawals at the homes or offices of specific customers. The consideration of whether a messenger service constitutes a branch is evaluated based on the factors set forth in OCC regulations (12 CFR 7.1012). If the messenger service is not considered to be a branch, it is not subject to branching limitations and approval by the OCC.

Alternatives to Branching

Assuming that a bank cannot, for legal or operational reasons, enter a particular locality through branching, a national bank may establish an office that engages in more limited activities and is not considered to be a branch. As a result, it is not subject to geographic restrictions or OCC approval. It may:

- Engage in loan origination. These are called loan production offices (LPOs). A national bank may engage in almost any activity involved in lending at an LPO, except disbursement of loan proceeds to borrowers.

- Loan proceeds must be disbursed through another mechanism, such as by:

  — Check through the mail.

  — Disbursal through a third-party escrow agent.

  — Crediting a deposit account of the borrower.

  Other methods of disbursal that do not trigger branching concerns also may be available.

- Engage in deposit production. These are called deposit production offices (DPOs). At a DPO, a national bank may open deposit accounts and engage in other activities related to the deposit account function, but may not take deposits from a depositor or pay withdrawals to a customer. Deposits and withdrawals must be made through other mechanisms, such as by mail or ATM machines.

- Establish an ATM or other form of unstaffed automated facility that customers may use to make deposits or receive withdrawals or loan proceeds. Automated facilities may be equipped with a telephone or televideo device that allows contact with bank personnel.

Since an LPO, DPO, or unstaffed automated facilities, such as ATMs, are not considered to be branches, any combination of these facilities at one location does not create a branch.[24]

Compliance Issues

All national banks, including tribally owned national banks, are subject to a number of statutes that are administered or enforced by the OCC. (See Appendix G for a list of related booklets that are included in the OCC's *Comptroller's Handbook*.) In addition to banking laws, national banks may be subject to various other federal, state, or tribal laws and regulations, including securities, insurance, fiduciary, consumer protection, and disclosure laws and regulations. For example, state or tribal contract law will apply to many transactions between a bank and its customers.

Because tribes interested in entering the national banking system have

---

[24] See 12 CFR 7.1003-1005 (LPOs), 12 CFR 7.4004 (DPOs), 12 CFR 7.4003 (unstaffed automated facilities), and 12 CFR 7.4005 (combinations) for more information.

questioned how certain statutes would be applied to tribally owned banks, this section includes a short discussion on:

- Fair lending.

- Community reinvestment.

- Securities.

- Bank secrecy and anti-money laundering.

Fair Lending Statutes

The federal fair lending statutes are the Equal Credit Opportunity Act (ECOA) and the Fair Housing Act (FH Act). The ECOA prohibits discrimination in any part of a credit transaction. The ECOA applies to any extension of credit, including extensions of credit to persons, small businesses, corporations, partnerships, and trusts. The FH Act applies to residential real-estate related transactions. Both of these acts prohibit discrimination based on race, color, religion, sex, or national origin. The ECOA also prohibits discrimination based on age, marital status, receipt of public assistance, or the exercise of a right under the Consumer Protection Act. The FH Act also prohibits discrimination based on handicap or familial status.

Generally, discrimination in a credit transaction against persons because they are (or are not) Native Americans violates the ECOA and, if the transaction is related to residential real estate, violates the FH Act. The ECOA, however, provides a limited exception to its general prohibition against discrimination when, to meet special social needs, a bank offers a special purpose credit program that conforms with the requirements in the FRB's Regulation B (12 CFR 202.8). The Department of Housing and Urban Development has indicated that a special purpose credit program meeting the requirements of Regulation B will also be allowed under the FH Act.

Community Reinvestment Act

Financial institutions are encouraged under the CRA to help meet the credit needs of their entire communities, consistent with the safe and sound operations of such institutions. Federal regulators rate banks and thrifts on how well they meet those credit needs. The regulator assigns a rating of "outstanding," "satisfactory," "needs to improve," or "substantial noncompliance" based on the bank's CRA performance.

The OCC takes into account a bank's record of helping to meet community credit needs in consideration of corporate applications for:

- The establishment of a domestic branch.

- The relocation of the main office or a branch.

- The merger of, or consolidation with, or the acquisition of assets or assumption of liabilities of an insured depository institution under the BMA.

- The conversion of an insured depository institution to a national bank charter.

The OCC's CRA regulation (12 CFR 25) establishes the framework and criteria by which the OCC will assess an institution's record of helping to meet the credit needs of its community. The CRA regulations provide different performance standards for assessing banks of different sizes and types. Large retail banks are evaluated based on their performance under three tests: a lending test, an investment test, and a service test. Wholesale and limited purpose banks are assessed under a community development test. Small institutions generally must meet the criteria of a streamlined small bank test. However, any bank can elect to be evaluated based on a strategic plan, developed with community input and approved by the OCC. Regardless of the performance test under which a national bank falls, examiners consider the bank's lending, qualified investments, and services.

The CRA regulation requires each bank to delineate at least one assessment area. A retail bank's assessment area(s) generally must consist of one or more metropolitan statistical areas (MSAs) or one or more contiguous political subdivisions, such as counties, cities, or towns. It must include the geographies[25] in which the bank has its main office, branches, and deposit-taking ATMs, as well as the surrounding geographies in which the bank has originated or purchased a substantial portion of its loans.[26] The federal financial institution supervisory agencies, including the OCC, have interpreted the term "political subdivision" to include Indian reservations.[27] A bank may adjust the boundaries of its assessment area(s) to include only the portion of a political subdivision that it reasonably can be expected to serve.

Each bank's assessment area(s):

---

[25]"Geography" is defined in the CRA regulation to mean a census tract or block numbering area delineated by the U.S. Bureau of the Census in the most recent decennial census. 12 CFR 25.12(l).

[26]12 CFR 25.41(c).

[27]Interagency Questions and Answers, 66 Fed. Reg. 36,620, 36,640-41 (July 12, 2001) (§ __.41(c)(1)-1).

- Must consist only of whole geographies.

- May not reflect illegal discrimination or redlining.

- May not arbitrarily exclude low- or moderate-income geographies, taking into account the bank's size and financial condition.

- May not extend substantially beyond a consolidated metropolitan statistical area boundary or beyond a state boundary, unless the assessment area is located in a multistate metropolitan statistical area.[28]

If a bank designates an Indian reservation as an assessment area, it should be aware that the reservation boundaries may not be consistent with those of the census tracts or block numbering areas (geographies) in the area. In that case, the bank must ensure that its assessment area consists only of whole geographies by adding any portions of the geographies that lie outside the Indian reservation to the delineated assessment area.[29]

A tribe that owns a bank located in a city outside of the reservation should also consider CRA assessment area requirements. The tribe, in this situation, should be aware that the bank's assessment area(s) must include the MSA or other political subdivision in which the bank's main office is located, its branches, and its deposit-taking ATMs.

(For more detailed information about compliance with consumer protection, fair lending,[30] and community reinvestment laws, see the pertinent booklets on consumer compliance in the *Comptroller's Handbook*. Appendix G explains how to obtain the booklets.)

Securities Laws

Offerings

Under the federal securities laws, the OCC reviews securities offering materials prepared by national banks. National banks seeking to sell or offer their securities must comply with both the applicable federal securities laws, including anti-fraud provisions, and OCC regulations. National banks must comply with those provisions when capitalizing a newly chartered bank, or when raising additional capital for their businesses and growth (12 CFR 16).

---

[28]12 CFR 25.41(d) and (e).

[29]Interagency Questions and Answers, 66 Fed. Reg. at 36,641 (§ __.41(c)(1)-1).

[30]See also Policy Statement on Discrimination in Lending, 59 Fed. Reg. 18,266 (April 15, 1994).

National bank securities offerings may be exempt from the registration requirements of the federal securities laws and the OCC's part 16. Such exemptions apply, for example, to nonpublic offerings and to small issues under the SEC's Regulation A. National banks should review 12 CFR 16.5 and relevant provisions of the federal securities laws to ensure that they structure those offerings to meet the requirements for an exemption from registration.

A national bank offering or selling its own securities in a particular state also may be subject to individual state laws governing the registration and sale of securities within the state (known popularly as "blue sky laws"). Tribally owned national banks should consult with bank counsel to determine whether they are subject to blue sky laws in a particular jurisdiction *before* selling securities.

Proxy Statements

The OCC reviews and clears *registered* banks' proxy or information statements before distribution to shareholders. A "registered" bank refers to a bank with assets of more than $1 million and with a class of stock owned by 500 or more persons. The OCC reviews proxy statements for material, substantive factual errors or omissions. Registered national banks must file proxy materials with the OCC when conducting/engaging in the following activities:

- A merger/consolidation when the resulting bank is a national bank.

- An election of bank directors.

- An annual or special shareholder meeting.

The OCC has incorporated by reference SEC regulations governing proxy solicitations and content at 12 CFR 11. Those regulations detail the information that banks must include in their proxy materials.

Bank Secrecy Act and Anti-Money Laundering Provisions

The Bank Secrecy Act (BSA) and its implementing regulations require financial institutions to file certain currency and monetary instrument reports and to maintain certain records for possible use in criminal, tax, and regulatory proceedings (31 USC 5311 et seq., 31 CFR 103, 12 CFR 21.21). Congress enacted the BSA to attempt to prevent financial institutions from being used as intermediaries for the movement of criminally derived funds to conceal the true source, ownership, or use of the funds, i.e., money laundering. Although attempts to launder money through a legitimate financial institution can emanate from many different sources, certain kinds of businesses, transactions, or geographic locations may lend themselves more readily to potential criminal activity than others.

All national banks must establish and maintain procedures reasonably designed to ensure and monitor their compliance with the BSA and its implementing regulations. This requires national banks to establish a compliance program that includes, at a minimum, adequate BSA policies and procedures, designation of a compliance officer, and BSA training and audits. In addition, national banks should be aware of various criminal statutes prohibiting money laundering and structuring of deposits to evade the BSA reporting requirements. (See 18 USC 1956, 1957 and 31 USC 5324.)

Banks must ensure that they have reasonable policies and procedures to verify the identity of people seeking to open an account at the bank as well as policies and procedures reasonably designed to detect suspicious activity. Each bank must file a Suspicious Activity Report (SAR) whenever it identifies:

- A known or suspected violation of law.

- A suspicious transaction that:

  - Has no business or apparent lawful purpose;

  - Is not the sort of transaction in which a particular customer normally would be expected to engage; **and**

  - Has no reasonable explanation for the transaction.

- A suspicious transaction that involves more than $5,000 in potential money laundering.

- A suspicious transaction that is an apparent attempt to evade the provisions of the BSA.

The SAR reporting requirements are provided in 12 CFR 21.11.

Financial Institution Charters and Regulators

Type of Charter	Primary Regulator(s)
National Bank	Office of the Comptroller of the Currency
State Member Bank[1]	State Bank Regulator and Federal Reserve Board (FRB)
State Non-Member Bank; State Savings Bank	State Bank Regulator and Federal Deposit Insurance Corporation (FDIC)
Federal Savings Association; Federal Savings Bank	Office of Thrift Supervision (OTS)
State Savings Association	State Bank Regulator and OTS
Bank Holding Company	FRB[2]
Savings Association Holding Company	OTS[3]
Federal Credit Union	National Credit Union Administration (NCUA)
State Credit Union	State Regulator and, where applicable by state law, NCUA[4]

[1] State banks can become members of the Federal Reserve System. National banks must be member banks.

[2] Depending on the state, bank and savings association holding companies also may be regulated by the state banking regulator and/or the state agency responsible for regulating corporate practices (e.g., Secretary of State).

[3] See footnote 2.

[4] Most states require state credit unions to be insured by the National Credit Union Administration, whose regulations governing insurance, therefore, would apply to such states' credit unions.

Roles of the Financial Regulators

- Contact the **Office of the Comptroller of the Currency** (OCC) for information about a national bank charter. To determine the appropriate office, see Appendix F for addresses and phone numbers. In addition, the OCC's *Comptroller's Licensing Manual* is available on the OCC's Web site (http://www.occ.treas.gov) in a searchable and downloadable format.

- Contact the **Office of Thrift Supervision** (OTS) for information about chartering a federal savings association or savings association holding company. To determine the appropriate regional office, see the OTS's Web site at http://ots.treas.gov or contact:

  OTS
  1700 G Street, NW
  Washington, DC 20552
  (202) 906-6000

- Contact the appropriate regional office of the **Federal Deposit Insurance Corporation** (FDIC) for information about federal deposit insurance for banks and savings associations. To determine the appropriate regional office, see the FDIC's Web site at http://www.fdic.gov or contact:

  FDIC
  550 17th Street, N.W.
  Washington, DC 20429
  (800) 276-6003 / (202) 416-6940

- Contact the appropriate **Federal Reserve Bank** for information about establishing a bank holding company or becoming a Fed member bank. To determine the appropriate office, see the Fed's Web site at http://www.federalreserve.gov or contact:

  Board of Governors of the Federal Reserve System
  20th and Constitution Avenue, N.W.
  Washington, DC 20551
  (202) 452-3000

- Contact the appropriate regional office of the **National Credit Union Administration** (NCUA) for information about chartering a federal credit union or obtaining deposit insurance. To determine the appropriate office, see NCUA's Web site at http://www.ncua.gov or contact:

NCUA
1775 Duke Street
Alexandria, Virginia 22314-3428
(703) 518-6330

Sample Commitment Letter

Date

Licensing Manager
Appropriate District Office
Street Address
City, State, ZIP Code

Re: Letter of Commitments for National Bank, City, State

Dear Licensing Manager:

Enclosed please find commitments pertaining to our application for a change in bank control of a national bank, city, state, pursuant to the Change in Bank Control Act (12 USC 1817(j)). Attached to these commitments are all requisite attachments, including all necessary Tribal resolutions and letters of counsel.

Definitions:

Tribe means, individually and collectively, [full name of Tribe] and any council, committee, division, office, commission, department, board, agency, authority, facility, instrumentality of [name of Tribe], or any other subordinate organization. Attached to these commitments is attachment A, which sets forth, as represented by the Tribe on this date, the name and each business activity of and/or other function performed by each such subordinate organization of the Tribe, and the relation of each such subordinate organization to, the Tribe, and which by this reference is incorporated.

Affiliate of the Tribe means, individually and collectively, any company that from time-to-time is controlled (as defined in the Board's Regulation O, 12 CFR 215.2(c)) by the Tribe, acting alone or in concert with one or more other persons (as defined in the Board's Regulation Y, 12 CFR 225.2(k)), but excluding any company identified and listed as a subordinate organization of the Tribe in attachment A or in a revised form of attachment A submitted to the Board pursuant to the following paragraph. Attached to these commitments is attachment B, which sets forth, as represented by the Tribe on this date, the name, address and business activity of each affiliate of the Tribe, and the equity interest of the Tribe, as of this date, and which by this reference is incorporated.

Bank means, individually and collectively, [bank being chartered, acquired, or controlled], and every other bank (as defined in section 2(c) of the Bank Holding Company Act), including any successor to the bank. "Bank" includes each company that from time-to-time is a subsidiary of the bank.

Banking law means:

- All federal, tribal, and state statutes, rules, and regulations that the Office of the Comptroller of the Currency (OCC), the Board of Governors of the Federal Reserve System (Board), the Federal Deposit Insurance Corporation (FDIC), the U.S. Department of Justice (DOJ), the U.S. Department of the Treasury (DOT), or any other federal banking agency or department (individually, a "federal banking authority" and, collectively, the "federal banking authorities") administers or for which such federal banking authority has rulemaking or enforcement authority, including without limitation, all provisions of Title 12, U.S. Code, as from time-to-time may be applicable to the bank, any institution-affiliated party (IAP) (as defined in sections 3(u) and 8(b)(3) of the Federal Deposit Insurance Act (FDIA)) thereof, the Tribe, or any affiliate of the Tribe.

- All federal criminal law violations that arise:

    — From the applicability of any provision of a banking law.

    — Under section 1001 of Title 18 of the U.S. Code as it relates to information, statements, omissions, writings, or reports to a federal banking authority.

    — Any other provision of Title 18 of the U.S. Code applicable to the ownership, control, operation or activities of a bank, bank holding company, or subsidiary thereof, or to the activities of any IAP for such bank, bank holding company or subsidiary.

    — The Bank Secrecy Act, or the Currency and Foreign Transactions Reporting Act.

- Any order or written agreement issued by any federal banking authority or an administrative law judge acting under authority delegated by any federal banking authority or federal court of competent jurisdiction pursuant to a banking law against or with bank, the Tribe, any affiliate of the Tribe, or any IAP.

Company means any corporation, partnership, business trust, association, or similar organization, including, but not limited to, those formed under Tribal statute.
Commitments

1. The Tribe agrees to waive and to cause each present and future affiliate of the Tribe to waive, any claim that a Tribal court has jurisdiction over, and the Tribe agrees not to assert sovereign immunity as a defense to, any matter, issue, dispute, investigation, action, subpoena, examination, or proceeding by any federal banking authority that arises as a result of Tribe's ownership interest of the bank. In all dealings of the Tribe or any affiliate of the Tribe with the bank, the Tribe will be deemed to be an IAP of the bank.

    Before consummation of the proposed acquisition of additional shares of the bank, the Tribe shall submit to the OCC:

    -   A properly executed and authenticated certificate of official action (including the relevant resolution) of the appropriate governing body of the Tribe, authorizing and directing the signatory designated by such entity to execute the commitments on its behalf, and by so doing to bind such entity to each provision of the commitments, including the waiver of any jurisdictional claim in any tribal court as provided in this commitment, to which the official seal or stamp of the Tribe, as the case may be, is affixed.

    -   One or more reasoned opinion of counsel, in a form satisfactory to the OCC, that the Tribe is authorized under all of its organizational and other governing documents (e.g., tribal constitution, bylaws, articles of incorporation, partnership agreements) to make, and the legal sufficiency of, the waiver of any jurisdictional claim in any tribal court, as provided in the commitment.

2. The Tribe agrees to provide, and agrees to cause any affiliate of the Tribe to provide, to the extent possible, all information, regardless of whether such information is located within or without the Tribe's territory (tribal territory), requested for any investigation, action, or proceeding by any federal banking authority relating to:

    -   Enforcement or possible enforcement of any banking law for any person or entity subject to it which arise from or relate to transactions of the bank.

    -   The ownership or control of the Tribe by the bank.

    -   The operations or activities of the bank, or any IAP, under the banking law, including any potential violation of law or regulation, any unsafe or unsound practice, or breach of fiduciary duty by the bank, or any IAP.
    -   The compliance of the Tribe and/or any affiliate with the provisions

of these commitments.

3.   The Tribe agrees to provide and to cause any affiliate of the Tribe to provide, to the extent possible, the OCC with access to, to permit the OCC to examine, and to provide, as requested, the OCC with copies of all books and records, and any other information of or concerning the Tribe and/or each affiliate of the Tribe regardless of whether such books, records, and other information is located within or without tribal territory, to the extent necessary to enable the OCC to examine fully the details of any transaction or series of transactions of the bank with the Tribe or any affiliate of the Tribe, directly or indirectly.

4.   In all dealings of the Tribe or any affiliate of the Tribe with the bank, the Tribe, and each affiliate of the Tribe and all insiders (as defined in the Board's Resolution, 12 CFR 215.2(h)), will be deemed to be insiders for purposes of the Board's Regulation O, 12 CFR Part 215, and the bank, and all insiders thereof, will comply with all requirements set out under the Board's Regulation O. In all such dealings, the Tribe and each affiliate of the Tribe will be deemed to be affiliates of the bank for purposes of sections 23A and 23B of the Federal Reserve Act, and the Tribe, each affiliate of the Tribe, and bank will comply with the requirements of sections 23A and 23B of the Federal Reserve Act applicable to affiliate of banks. The bank will not, directly or indirectly, make any extension of credit to the Tribe or to any affiliate of the Tribe, including the issuance of a commercial or standby letter of credit or guarantee for the benefit of the Tribe or any affiliate of the Tribe, in an amount exceeding the applicable limits of, or in a manner inconsistent with, the requirements regarding extensions of credit subject to sections 12 USC 375a, 375b, 1817(k), and 1972 and implementing regulations set forth at 12 CFR parts 31 and 215. For purposes of this commitment, any transaction, including any extension of credit, with a third party shall be deemed to be a transaction with the Tribe or an affiliate of the Tribe to the extent that the proceeds of the transaction are used for the benefit of, or are transferred to the Tribe or an affiliate of the Tribe.

5.   The Tribe agrees to submit to the OCC revised attachment A and/or B to reflect any change in the information contained in attachment A and/or B, and a statement of the reasons for such change, within 30 days after any such change and annually, or upon the request of OCC staff. Should an entity become a subordinate organization or an affiliate of the Tribe and remain as such before the Tribe submits a revised notice as previously described, any such event shall be reported to the OCC within 30 days of any change. All commitments shall apply in full to any entity that becomes a subordinate organization or an affiliate of the Tribe after this date, immediately upon such entity satisfying the definitions of such terms in Part 1 hereof, as if such entity were a

subordinate organization or an affiliate of the Tribe, as the case may be, on this date. All such notices shall be submitted to the OCC together with one or more reasoned opinions of counsel that the subordinate organization of the Tribe or the affiliate of the Tribe, as the case may be, is authorized under all of its organizational and other governing documents (e.g., tribal constitution, bylaws, articles of incorporation, partnership agreement) to make, and the legal sufficiency of, each of the commitments including the waiver of any jurisdiction of any tribal court, as provided in commitment one.

Attached, and in which this reference is incorporated, is a properly executed and authenticated certificate of a tribal resolution authorizing the signatory to execute the commitments.

Full Name of Tribe

(Signature of Tribal Chief or other tribal official with authority to sign on behalf of the Tribe)

Printed or typed name of Tribal Chief or other tribal official

Explanatory Information about Commitments

Commitment One

This commitment assures the OCC that the Tribe will be subject to the federal banking laws and that enforcement of those laws will be administered by the federal court system. The commitment also assures the OCC that the Tribe has the authority under its own laws to enter into these commitments and has done so consistent with those laws.

Commitment Two

This commitment assures the OCC of ready access to information, such as loan documentation, shareholder lists, or transaction data, that the agency might require during an examination or investigation of the bank or parties affiliated with the bank.

Commitment Three

This commitment is required for reasons similar to those for requiring commitment two. Commitment three, however, references specifically books and records as they are often the subject of examinations, investigations, and other supervisory or enforcement proceedings.

Commitment Four

This commitment clarifies the applicability to the Tribe and its affiliates of statutes and regulations concerning loans to insiders and transactions with affiliates. These statutes and regulations will be applied to Tribes in a manner no different than they are applied to organizations, such as partnerships, corporations, banks, and bank holding companies, or to the affiliates of any of these organizations.

Commitment Five

This commitment outlines the process by which the Tribe will keep the OCC informed of changes in its organization's structure or its affiliation with other entities. The commitment also ensures the OCC that any changes in the organizational structure of the Tribe will not impair the applicability or enforceability of the commitments to the Tribe, its subordinate organizations, or its affiliates. Finally, the commitments assure the OCC that the actions taken by representatives for the Tribe have been properly executed, authenticated, and signed.

Comptroller of the Currency
Administrator of National Banks

Washington, DC 20219

October 3, 2001

To: Prospective Community Development Bank Organizing Groups

From: Julie L. Williams, First Senior Deputy Comptroller and Chief
            Counsel

Subject: Community Development (CD) Banks

The Comptroller of the Currency (OCC) receives numerous inquiries and
proposals from individuals and groups expressing interest in establishing a
CD bank to conduct new business or converting existing operations into a CD
bank. The purpose of this memorandum is to outline the criteria the OCC
uses in granting a CD bank charter, explain the assistance OCC may provide
to organizers of CD banks, and state the factors the OCC considers to be
critical to the success of any de novo CD bank.

What Is a CD Bank?

A CD bank is a depository institution with a stated mission primarily to
benefit the underserved communities in which it is chartered to conduct
business. A CD bank pursues this specialized mission by providing financial
services to low- and moderate-income (LMI) individuals or communities or
benefiting other areas targeted for redevelopment by local, state, tribal, or
federal government.

The OCC grants a special CD designation to banks that intend primarily to
engage in these CD activities. The bank's articles of association must indicate
the express intent primarily to lend, invest, and provide services in the
underserved communities in which it is chartered to conduct business. The

OCC designates a bank as a CD bank after a review of the charter application (*de novo* CD bank) or business plan (conversion to a CD bank). CD banks must meet the same safety and soundness, statutory, regulatory, business planning, and procedural requirements as all other national banks.

Applying for a CD Bank Charter

For organizers of de novo CD banks, the guidelines for applying for a national bank charter are outlined in the following OCC publications, which are available on the OCC's Web site and from the OCC's district licensing offices (locations and telephone numbers are also available in the "Licensing Applications" section of the OCC's Web site at www.occ.treas.gov):

- *A Guide to the National Banking System*

- *Comptroller's Licensing Manual* in booklets dealing with:

    - Charters (*de novo* and conversions)
    - Corporate Organization
    - General Policies and Procedures
    - Background Investigations
    - Public Involvement

- *A Guide to Tribal Ownership of a National Bank*

In addition to the required submissions outlined in these publications, CD banks must provide to the OCC a proposal describing how and why the bank is eligible for and seeking the CD designation with specific information documenting:

- How the bank's activities will primarily benefit LMI individuals, LMI areas, or other areas targeted for redevelopment by local, state, tribal, or the federal government, and

- The nature of the nonbank community involvement.

How Can National Banks Invest in CD Banks?

A national bank may make an investment in a CD bank either under the statute and regulation pertaining to community development corporations (CDCs), CD projects, and other public welfare investments (12 USC 24 (Eleventh) and 12 CFR Part 24), or under its broad authority to engage in the business of banking and activities incidental thereto (12 USC 24 (Seventh)). A bank may also receive credit under the Community Reinvestment Act (CRA) for investing in a CD bank.

A national bank may make an investment pursuant to the provisions of 12 USC 24 (Eleventh), provided that the CD bank's loans, investments, and services primarily benefit LMI individuals, LMI areas, or other areas targeted for redevelopment by state, local, tribal, or the federal government by providing or supporting one or more of the items listed below:

- Affordable housing, community services, or permanent jobs for LMI individuals

- Equity or debt financing for small businesses

- Area revitalization or stabilization

- Other activities, services, or facilities that primarily promote the public welfare

National banks seeking to make an investment in a CD bank under this authority should follow the procedures outlined in 12 CFR Part 24 (information is available on the Community Affairs page of OCC's Web site under "Publications and Resource Materials"). It should be noted that, typically, a national bank's total investment under the Part 24 authority is limited to 5 percent of its capital and unimpaired surplus, although it may go as high as 10 percent, with OCC approval.

Alternatively, a national bank may make a noncontrolling investment in a CD bank following the provisions of 12 USC 24 (Seventh), provided that the following provisions of 12 CFR 5.36 are met:

- The activities of the CD bank in which the investment is made must be limited to activities that are part of, or incidental to, the business of banking (or otherwise authorized for a national bank).

- The investing bank must be able to prevent the CD bank from engaging in activities that do not meet the foregoing standard, or be able to withdraw its investment.

- The investment in the CD bank is convenient and useful to the investing bank in carrying out its business and not a mere passive investment unrelated to the bank's banking business.

- The investing bank's loss exposure in the CD bank must be limited, as a legal and accounting matter, and the bank must not have open-ended liability for the obligations of the enterprise.

Regardless of which investment authority is used, an investing bank that would have a significant ownership interest in a CD bank should consult the Federal Reserve to determine whether its investment would cause the investing bank to be deemed a bank holding company under the Bank Holding Company Act.

Can National Banks Purchase Subordinated Debt of CD Banks?

National banks may invest in subordinated debt of a CD bank. Such investment may be eligible as Tier 2 capital for the CD bank and thus can enhance a CD bank's ability to supplement its capital base. However, it should be noted that the inclusion of term subordinated debt in Tier 2 capital is limited to 50 percent of the CD bank's Tier 1 capital (see appendix A of 12 CFR Part 3).

How Can State-Chartered Banks and Bank Holding Companies Invest in CD Banks?

State-chartered banks may be able to invest in CD banks pursuant to the Federal Reserve Board's Regulation H (for state member banks) or the FDIC's rules set forth at 12 CFR Part 362 (for state nonmember banks). Bank holding companies also may be able to make investments in CD banks following the provisions of the Federal Reserve Board's Regulation Y. The Federal Deposit Insurance Corporation (FDIC) can provide more information about 12 CFR Part 362. The Federal Reserve Board or the Federal Reserve Banks (FRB) can provide more information about Regulations H and Y.

Technical Assistance Available to CD Bank Organizers

The OCC provides technical assistance upon request to the organizers of *de novo* CD banks, during the charter exploratory, planning, and pre-filing period. An OCC team of licensing, supervision, legal, and community affairs staff is available to meet with organizers to provide information and feedback on issues related to a *de novo* bank's proposed business plan and CD focus. The OCC encourages prospective applicants to contact the OCC's district licensing staff that serves the area in which the bank will be located to discuss corporate proposals.

After these initial discussions, groups that have explored all charter and community development aspects of their application are encouraged to submit a draft application to the OCC prior to the submission of their formal application. The OCC considers it important that the initial draft be as complete as possible.

For a listing of phone numbers and more detailed information on the specifics of the application requirements and timeframes, please visit the "Licensing Applications" page of the OCC's Web site.

Key Factors to Consider When Organizing a CD Bank

It is the OCC's policy to approve proposals to establish national banks that will operate in a safe and sound manner and have a reasonable chance of success. The OCC's decision whether or not to grant a new charter application depends on an assessment of the organizing group's qualifications, choice of management and directors, and the strength of its business plan, including capitalization, contingency planning, and financial projections.

CD banks face unique challenges in accomplishing the dual objectives of being profitable institutions operated in a safe and sound manner and fulfilling their mission to focus on activities that promote the public welfare. Based on the OCC's experience working with CD banks that have been chartered and are now in business, the agency has identified the following areas deserving special attention by entities seeking to establish or convert to a CD bank.

Contact with Community Organizations

It is important that, early in the process of organizing or converting to a CD bank, organizers meet with local community organizations to engage them in a dialogue on CD needs in the geographic area in which the bank will be operating. This will help determine local community credit needs, which must be demonstrated as part of any de novo bank charter application or existing bank's conversion to a CD focus. The OCC would view positively an organizing group that has strong ties in the community where it wishes to operate the bank.

Diversified Asset Base and Income Stream

Organizers must consider how a *de novo* institution will operate in a safe and sound manner, given its CD focus. Often, this means the bank's plans should serve both a broader market as well as its primary CD-focus market in order to lay a broad foundation for its future operations. Diversified asset and liability portfolios, product selection, funding sources, and target markets help make a bank less vulnerable to a downturn in any one market that could significantly affect its income or liquidity.

In the early stages, organizers of CD banks likely will need to develop a business plan that addresses not only the underserved communities that are its special focus but also more traditional, full service retail banking activities. These services may encompass a wider geographical area than a CD bank's targeted communities, particularly in the early years of operation. During this "ramping-up" period, this mix of business can help a CD bank to grow into a healthy and profitable institution while still meeting its overall mission of serving targeted areas. An exclusive focus on underserved markets in a CD bank's early years simply may not generate enough business to enable the *de novo* institution to become viable and may subject it to a higher risk profile than desirable. The ramping-up period will vary depending upon the bank's business plan, as well as economic and market conditions, and may last for several years.

Capital Adequacy

The OCC's chartering policy in 12 CFR 5.20 states that a proposed bank must have capital sufficient to protect against the various risks inherent in the bank's business plan. This initial capital raised is net of organizing expenses that will be charged to the bank's capital after it begins operations. An organizing group must therefore raise a sufficient amount of capital to pay all organization costs, compete effectively in the market area, and support planned operations adequately. Additionally, initial capitalization must be sufficient to maintain adequate capital levels until the bank achieves profitable operations. A *de novo* CD bank's business plan should also identify sufficient capital to address uncertainties in the marketplace and should demonstrate a clear ability to raise additional capital, if needed.

The OCC has not formally established a minimum capital level for *de novo* banks. The initial capital plan of a CD bank is reviewed against the bank's business plan to determine if the proposed capital will be sufficient to support the projected volume and type of business the organizing group has proposed. The OCC, as the primary supervisor of national banks, will require proposed banks, including CD banks, with higher risk profiles to have higher capital reserves than proposed banks that present lower risk. For example, recent CD bank charter approvals have presented capital plans in the range of $6.2 million to $7.5 million with various applications incorporating different risk factors. The FDIC requires that, as a condition of granting deposit insurance, *de novo* banks maintain a Tier 1 capital-to-assets ratio of not less than 8 percent through the first three years of operation. (See ▯▯ ▯▯ ▯▯▯▯e▯ en▯ o▯ ▯o▯▯▯ on ▯ ▯ ▯▯▯▯on▯ ▯o▯ ▯ e▯ o▯▯ ▯n▯▯ ▯▯ n▯e at www.fdic.gov/lawsregs/rules/5000-9.html.)

Financial Assistance from the Community Development Financial Institutions (CDFI) Fund

The Treasury Department's CDFI Fund can provide additional sources of financial assistance for CD banks under the two programs described as follows. However, organizers of CD banks should understand key provisions of these programs, specifically, how they may limit flexibility or otherwise affect the bank. Information on these programs may be obtained from the Treasury Department Web site located at www.treas.gov/cdfi.

Core Component Program: This program builds the financial capacity of CDFIs by providing equity investments, grants, loans, or deposits to enhance the capital base of CDFIs. In addition, under the Core Component Program, technical assistance grants are provided to CDFIs to build their capacity to address the CD needs of their target markets.

Bank Enterprise Award program: The BEA program provides monetary incentives for banks and thrifts to expand their investments in CDFIs or to increase their lending, investment, and service activities in distressed communities. BEA monies are awarded on a competitive basis to institutions that apply for the funds and meet agreed-upon performance goals.

Bank Management/Board of Directors

The OCC requires each organizer to have a history of responsibility, personal honesty, and integrity. While personal wealth is not a requirement for a bank organizer or director, poor management of personal financial affairs will have a negative impact on the OCC's decision. Additional information on these topics can be found in the OCC's booklet on "Background Investigations" in the "Corporate Policies" section of the *Comptroller's Licensing Manual* and on the OCC's Web site.

The management team of a CD bank should demonstrate the experience, competence, and willingness to operate a CD-focused institution. Organizers should recognize that the selection of a qualified CEO is one of the most important decisions they will make. The risks associated with a CD bank require that the proposed CEO be actively involved in developing the business plan, have strong leadership skills, and be an experienced banking executive. The CEO should have skills that complement those of the directors and other proposed members of the executive officer team. Also, the unique characteristics of a CD bank business plan and the specific needs of its customers often require the management team to be comprised of individuals who understand CD and have worked with the LMI community.

Likewise, CD bank directors should have a balance of banking experience and knowledge of local community credit needs in order to keep the institution focused on becoming profitable while fulfilling its mission. It is vitally important that proposed directors of *de novo* CD banks fully understand and be committed to the institution's proposed business plan. Given the great importance of selecting proper management and directors, the OCC suggests early discussions with its staff for guidance regarding best practices in the selection process. Many problems may be avoided when care is exercised in this process.

The proposed management team must, either individually or collectively, possess extensive knowledge and experience with the highly specialized lending products and lines of business typically proposed by CD banks (e.g.,

Small Business Administration and Federal Housing Administration programs). An organizing group should match carefully the skills of the management team to the specialized lending products and services that the CD bank will offer.

General information about the role of directors can be obtained in 𝑡𝑡e 𝑡𝑡e𝑡𝑡o𝑡𝑡 𝑡oo𝑡𝑡𝑡 e 𝑡 o𝑡e o𝑡 𝑡 𝑡𝑡on𝑡𝑡𝑡 n 𝑡 𝑡e𝑡𝑡o𝑡 (available on the "Publications" page of OCC's Web site).

Partnerships with Other Banks

Other financial institutions that invest in a CD bank may be operating in the same market and have considerable experience and talent to offer in an advisory role to that CD bank. Investor institutions are able to assist CD banks in a number of ways, including

- Providing an "officer-on-loan" for temporary training assistance

- Consulting and training on operations, and

- Establishing two-way referral/correspondent relationships on loan business.

The OCC encourages CD banks to learn as much as they can from investor banks that have developed CD banking expertise in similar markets and lines of business.

However, the OCC has often seen bank investors conclude their relationships with a CD bank after providing initial capital, perhaps because of perceived prohibitions under the Depository Institutions Management Interlocks Act (DIMIA) (12 USC 3201 e𝑡 𝑡e𝑡 𝑡) which generally prohibits management officials from serving on the board of directors of an unaffiliated bank. While these regulations should be researched based on the specific circumstances, there are some exceptions that may be available. These exceptions allow management officials of an established bank to serve on the board of an unaffiliated CD bank that provides services in an LMI area, is minority- or women-owned, or is newly chartered. In cases where a management official of a national bank seeks to serve on the board of an unaffiliated CD bank, the bank may request the OCC to grant a waiver from the DIMIA restrictions. Such requests must be made in writing to the OCC's licensing staff and, where appropriate, are normally granted for three years for established banks and two years for *de novo* banks.

There is also a "small market share" exemption to the DIMIA management interlock restrictions where the two "interlocking" banks together hold less than 20 percent of the deposits in their community or relevant metropolitan statistical area. Banks need not seek OCC approval for this exemption but they must maintain records to support their qualification for this exemption.

Representatives of banks also may serve on an advisory board or as an honorary director of a CD bank, provided that the CD bank's total assets are less than $100 million. If a CD bank's assets exceed this level, then the interlock provisions (and exceptions) described above would apply.

A bank investor in a CD bank that seeks to place one of its management officials on the board of a CD bank should also consult the Board of Governors of the Federal Reserve System or the Federal Reserve Banks concerning certain prohibitions under the FRB's Bank Holding Company Act rules and interpretations governing control of banks.

Funding and Liquidity

Some CD banks have found that lending and investing needs in their target communities exceed available core deposits in these areas. Consequently, some CD banks have turned to philanthropic and corporate investors located outside of their service areas to make deposits in the bank. There may be higher costs associated with reliance on these types of funding sources (see the "Liquidity" booklet of the 🔲 o🔲 🔲🔲o🔲e🔲🔲 🔲 nd🔲oo🔲 which is available on the "Publications" page of the OCC's Web site). CD banks relying on these types of funds should be prepared to document to their examiners the sources of these funds and the degree to which these funds demonstrate credit and rate sensitivity. CD banks should have contingency plans to replace these funding sources if the deposits are withdrawn.

CD Banks' CRA Evaluation

CD banks are evaluated under the same CRA criteria as all other community banks. Holding a CD charter is not a guarantee of an "Outstanding" CRA rating. Organizers, management, and directors should recognize that, due to the unique risks associated with a CD bank's niche market, the institution may need to pursue its CD mission by gradually ramping up its CD activities in order to concentrate on the fundamentals of safety and soundness, prudent growth, and profitability during its early years. Thus, a CD bank's CRA performance may not be as strong in its early years as it will become as its business and marketing plan develops.

Communications with the OCC

Responsibility for the direction and management of a CD bank rests with the bank's board of directors and senior management team. The OCC's national bank examiners (NBEs) and district community affairs officers (DCAOs) will not participate in setting policies or directing the bank.

However, given CD banks' unique challenge to be profitable institutions, operate in a safe and sound manner, and fulfill their CD mission, the OCC encourages CD banks to maintain an ongoing dialogue with their NBEs and DCAOs. As part of the OCC's supervisory process and through quarterly reviews of bank performance, the OCC will work with CD banks to identify risks to the bank and suggest methods of approaching potential problems. As part of the supervisory process, the OCC will provide information on compliance, risk management, and operational issues facing the bank. Experts are also available in each district to provide guidance on subjects such as credit and asset management, consumer compliance, capital markets, bank information systems, legal issues, and economic conditions.

Comptroller of the Currency
Administrator of National Banks

Washington, DC 20219

Office of the Comptroller of the Currency

Policy Statement on Minority-Owned National Banks

Recognizing the important role that minority-owned banks play in addressing financial services needs in the minority and low-income communities they serve, the Office of the Comptroller of the Currency (OCC) affirms its commitment to encouraging the success of these banks. Consistent with the goals of Section 308 of the Financial Institutions Reform, Recovery, and Enforcement Act of 1989 (FIRREA), which include preserving existing minority depository institutions and promoting the creation of new minority depository institutions, this statement outlines OCC policies and initiatives that further the ability of minority banks to prosper and meet the needs of their communities. These policies complement the OCC's overall mission of ensuring a safe, sound, and competitive banking system.

Definition of Minority-Owned Banks

OCC's definition of minority-owned bank is consistent with that established by the Treasury Department for eligibility in the Minority Bank Deposit Program and includes minority-owned or controlled banks as well as banks owned, controlled, and operated by women.

Identification of Minority-Owned Banks

OCC will annually identify minority-owned national banks that participate in the Treasury Department's Minority Bank Deposit Program. OCC will maintain a list of minority-owned national banks and make it available on lon   n ne and the OCC's Web site to entities interested in establishing business relationships with minority-owned institutions.

Formation of Minority-Owned Banks

The OCC provides advice and technical assistance to minority bank applicants interested in entering the national banking system. A national bank whose mission focuses on low- and moderate-income individuals or areas or government revitalization areas may be eligible for designation as a community development focus bank which would facilitate investments by other depository institutions. The OCC has produced materials geared to minority bank organizers, which facilitate the development of national bank applications. The OCC also provides assistance to organizers of minority institutions through pre-filing meetings and comments on draft applications. Requests for such assistance should be directed to the licensing manager in the OCC's district office that serves the area in which the bank will be headquartered.

Capital for Minority-Owned Banks

Investments in minority-owned banks are allowable investments pursuant to 12 USC 24(Eleventh) and 12 CFR Part 24 ("Part 24"), depending on the nature of the minority institution's mission and business operations, and may also be eligible for positive consideration under the Community Reinvestment Act. Receiving a community development focus designation, or otherwise engaging in activities authorized by Part 24, may further enhance access to capital for a minority-owned national bank by helping to establish its eligibility for funding from the Community Development Financial Institutions Fund of the Treasury Department.

OCC's Community Affairs Department can provide technical assistance to minority-owned institutions interested in structuring community development investments under Part 24. In addition, the Community Affairs Department can assist an established minority-owned bank in seeking designation as a community development focus bank.

Examination Support for Minority-Owned Banks

As part of its supervisory process and through quarterly reviews of bank performance, OCC examiners communicate regularly with minority bankers to identify risks to the bank and suggest methods of approaching any potential problems. As part of the supervisory process, OCC examiners also will provide information on compliance, risk management, and operational issues facing the bank. Experts also are available in each district to provide guidance on subjects such as credit and asset management, consumer compliance, capital markets, bank information systems, legal issues, and economic conditions.

The OCC will provide examination continuity for minority-owned national banks through the assignment of a portfolio manager who will have familiarity with the bank. Assignments of examiners to minority-owned banks will take into account the expertise and background needed to properly evaluate the products and services offered by those institutions and the markets and environments in which they operate.

Information, Education and Outreach for Minority-Owned Banks

Minority-owned national banks will be invited to attend outreach meetings throughout the country to discuss supervisory and industry issues with OCC personnel. In addition, the OCC will sponsor roundtable discussions or conferences for CEOs and senior managers of minority-owned national banks to highlight "best practices" and issues of particular relevance to minority-owned institutions. When feasible, OCC staff also will participate in other seminars, conferences and workshops directed to minority-owned institution audiences.

The OCC will promote the use of the Comparative Analysis Reporting system on ☐ ☐☐on☐ ☐ n☐ ne☐ by minority-owned national banks. A minority-owned national bank can use this system to develop peer group analyses that help the bank to identify its relative strengths and weaknesses by comparing its performance to other specified banks or groups of banks. The system includes publicly available call report data on all Federal Deposit Insurance Corporation (FDIC)-insured banks.

Supervisory Cases

When supervisory cases entail resolving a minority-owned national bank, the OCC will work with the FDIC and will provide the necessary support to enable the FDIC to identify potential minority investors. The OCC encourages the preservation of the minority character of institutions in cases involving mergers or acquisitions.

_____/s/_____
John D. Hawke, Jr.
Comptroller of the Currency

March 28, 2001

OCC Contacts

General Information

Office of the Comptroller of the Currency
250 E Street, S.W.
Washington, DC 20219-0001

Telephone   (202) 874-5000
Web site   http://www.occ.treas.gov

Headquarters Divisions of Interest to Tribes Forming National Banks

Asset Management

Telephone   (202) 874-4447
Fax Number   (202) 874-9390

Has responsibility for the development and coordination of supervisory
policies for national banks' asset management activities, including traditional
fiduciary activities, investment advisory services, and the retail sale of
nondeposit products.

Bank Activities and Structure

Telephone   (202) 874-5300
Fax Number   (202) 874-5322

Has responsibility for legal issues relating to banking organizations and
structures and various banking activities.

Licensing
Telephone   (202) 874-5060
Fax Number   (202) 874-5293
Web site   bos@occ.treas.gov

Processes licensing applications from all national bank subsidiaries of certain
holding companies assigned to the Washington, DC licensing unit, and
applications involving novel, complex, or precedent-setting issues. Also has
responsibility for oversight of district Licensing staff and development and

implementation of licensing policies.

Banking Relations

Telephone   (202) 874-4990
Fax Number   (202) 874-5305

Builds and maintains bridges with financial services industry stakeholders, primarily commercial banks and their representatives, for a constructive exchange of information integral to OCC policy creation and implementation.

Communications

Telephone   (202) 874-4700
Subscriptions   (202) 874-4960
Fax Number   (202) 874-5263

Provides publications support and information services for the agency, including responding to inquiries from the public about the agency's mission and activities, operating and overseeing the Public Information Room, which offers access to OCC public documents, and processing all initial requests filed under the Freedom of Information and Privacy Acts.

Compliance

Telephone   (202) 874-4428
Fax Number   (202) 874-5221

Has responsibility for compliance and CRA examinations as well as community and consumer policy issues, including designation of limited purpose banks under 12 CFR 25.

Community Affairs

Telephone   (202) 874-5556
Fax Number   (202) 874-4652

Has responsibility for community development policy issues, including filings under 12 CFR 24, and national level initiatives encouraging investment, lending, and services to low- and moderate-income persons and communities and small businesses. Also has responsibility for the OCC's outreach and external relations with consumer and community organizations, as well as national and regional civil rights and minority-based organizations, particularly those concerned with access to financial services.

Community and Consumer Law

Telephone   (202) 874-5750
Fax Number   (202) 874-5322

Has responsibility for community and consumer legal issues, including community reinvestment and community development (CD) matters.

Ombudsman

Comptroller of the Currency
301 McKinney Street, Suite 3725
Houston, Texas 77010-3034

Telephone   (713) 336-4350
Fax Number   (713) 336-4351

Has responsibility for overseeing the national bank appeals process and the customer assistance group.

Securities and Corporate Practices

Telephone   (202) 874-5210
Fax Number   (202) 874-5279

Has responsibility for securities, derivatives, capital markets, fiduciary, and insurance legal issues, as well as corporate governance and shareholder rights.

OCC District Offices

Northeastern

Licensing Manager
1114 Avenue of the Americas, Suite 3900
New York, New York 10036-7780

Telephone   (212) 790-4055
Fax Number   (212) 790-4058

Supervises most national banks headquartered in Connecticut, Delaware, District of Columbia, Maine, Maryland, Massachusetts, New Hampshire, New Jersey, New York, Pennsylvania, Puerto Rico, Rhode Island, Vermont, and the Virgin Islands.

Southeastern

Licensing Manager
Marquis One Tower, Suite 600
245 Peachtree Center Ave., N.E.
Atlanta, Georgia 30303-1223

Telephone   (404) 588-4525
Fax Number   (404) 588-4544

Supervises most national banks headquartered in Alabama, Florida, Georgia, Mississippi, North Carolina, South Carolina, Tennessee, Virginia, and West Virginia.

Central

Licensing Manager
One Financial Place, Suite 2700
440 South LaSalle Street
Chicago, Illinois 60605-1073

Telephone   (312) 360-8851
Fax Number   (312) 435-0951

Supervises most national banks headquartered in Illinois, Indiana, Kentucky, Michigan, Ohio, and Wisconsin.

Midwestern

Licensing Manager
2345 Grand Boulevard, Suite 700
Kansas City, Missouri 64108-2637

Telephone   (816) 556-1860
Fax Number   (816) 556-1892

Supervises most national banks headquartered in Iowa, Kansas, Minnesota, Missouri, Nebraska, North Dakota, and South Dakota.

Southwestern

Licensing Manager
500 North Akard Street, Suite 1600
Dallas, Texas 75201-3342

| Telephone | (214) 720-7052 |
| Fax Number | (214) 720-7068 |

Supervises most national banks headquartered in Arkansas, Louisiana, Oklahoma, and Texas.

Western

Licensing Manager
50 Fremont Street, Suite 3900
San Francisco, California 94105-2292

| Telephone | (415) 545-5916 |
| Fax Number | (415) 442-5315 |

Supervises most national banks headquartered in Alaska, Arizona, California, Colorado, Guam, Hawaii, Idaho, Montana, Nevada, New Mexico, Northern Mariana Islands, Oregon, Washington, Wyoming, and Utah.

District Community Affairs Officers (DCAOs)

Washington Office

District Community Affairs Director
Telephone   (202) 874-4851
Fax Number   (202) 874-5566

Has responsibility for facilitating partnerships; providing technical assistance for banks and their community partners; and encouraging investment, lending, and services to low- and moderate-income persons and small businesses. The DCAOs provide training and advice to national banks, communities, and bank examiners on best practices, options for satisfying CRA responsibilities, and how to expand access to credit and capital.

DCAOs

Northeastern District

| John Farrell | (617) 424-4994 | fax (617) 424-4992 |
| Denise Kirk-Murray | (212) 790-4054 | fax (212) 790-4098 |

Southeastern District

| Karol Klim | (404) 588-4515 | fax (404) 588-4532 |
| Nancy Gresham-Jones | (404) 588-4515 | fax (404) 588-4532 |

Central District

Paul Ginger	(312) 360-8876	fax (312) 435-0951

Midwestern District

Annette Lepique	(816) 556-1832	fax (816) 556-1892

Southwestern District

David Lewis	(214) 720-7027	fax (214) 720-7017
David Miller	(214) 720-7067	fax (214) 720-7017

Western District

Julia Brown	(415) 545-5956	fax (415) 545-5974
Susan Howard	(818) 240-9192	fax (818) 240-9690

A Guide to Tribal Ownership
of a National Bank

OCC Publications

OCC publications that you may find useful are listed in this Appendix. To request an order form and list of publications, contact the OCC's Communications Division at (202) 874-4700 or visit the OCC's Web site at http://www.occ.treas.gov.

Comptroller's Licensing Manual (all booklets listed)

Introduction
General Policies and Procedures
Background Investigations
Corporate Organization
Public Involvement
Charters
Conversions
Federal Branches and Agencies
Branches and Relocations
Business Combinations
Failure Acquisitions
Fiduciary Powers
Investment in Subsidiaries and Equities
Branch Closings
Capital and Dividends
Change in Bank Control
Changes in Directors and Senior Executive Officers
Changes of Corporate Title and Address
Comments to Other Agencies
Director Waivers
Investment in Bank Premises
Management Interlocks
Subordinated Debt
Termination of National Bank Status

Other Publications

The Internet and the National Bank Charter
A Guide to the National Banking System
A Guide to Tribal Ownership of a National Bank

OCC Booklets Handbook

Supervision booklets (selected booklets listed)
    Bank Supervision Process
    Community Bank Supervision
    Insider Activities
    Internal and External Audits
    Internal Control
    Large Bank Supervision
    Litigation and Other Legal Matters
    Management Information Systems

Compliance booklets (selected booklets listed)

    Bank Secrecy Act/Anti-Money Laundering
    Community Bank Consumer Compliance
    Community Reinvestment Act Examination Procedures
    Compliance Management System
    Fair Lending Examination Procedures
    Overview [of Compliance booklets]

Asset Management booklets

    Asset Management
    Community Bank Fiduciary Activities Supervision
    Conflicts of Interest
    Custody Services
    Investment Management Services

Other OCC Publications

"Activities Permissible for A National Bank" on the OCC's Web site, which is updated periodically.

A Guide to Community Lending in Indian Country, Comptroller of the Currency, July 1997.

"Banking in Indian Country – Challenges and Opportunities," *Community Development*, Fall 2001.

Community Development Banking, October 2001 Memorandum to Prospective Community Development Bank Organizing Groups. (See Appendix D.)

Community Development Investments and Resource Directory, Comptroller of the Currency, December 1996.

"Community Development Financial Institutions and CD Banks – Natural Partners for Traditional Lenders," *□o□ □□n□□□ □eve□o□□en□□*, Summer 2002.

CDFI and CD Bank Web Resource Directory available at http://www.occ.treas.gov/cdd/cdresourcedir.htm.

□□e □□e□□o□□□oo□□□□e □o□e o□□□e □□□on□□□□n□ □□e□□o□□ Comptroller of the Currency, March 1997.

Native American Banking Resource Directory available at http://ww.occ.treas.gov/cdd/nativeam.htm.

Policy Statement on Minority-Owned National Banks, March 2001. (See Appendix E).

□□ov□d□n□ □□n□n□□□□e□v□□e□□o□ □□□ve □□□e□□□n□□n□□nd□□n□□o□n□□□ Comptroller of the Currency, July 1997.

A Guide to Tribal Ownership
of a National Bank

Resource Contacts

Office of Tribal Justice
Department of Justice
Room 5634 Main Justice Building
950 Pennsylvania Avenue, N.W.
Washington, DC 20530-0001
(202) 514-8812
Web site: http://www.usdoj.gov/otj/index.html

Federal Programs

Federal Housing Finance Board
Affordable Housing and Community Investment Programs
1777 F Street, N.W.
Washington, DC 20006
(202) 408-2537
Web site: http://www.fhfb.gov

Department of Agriculture
Rural Development
1400 Independence Avenue, S.W.
Washington, DC 20250
(202) 720-4323
Web site: http://www.rurdev.usda.gov

Department of Commerce
Economic Development Administration
14th Street and Constitution Avenue, N.W., Room 7804
Washington, DC 20230
(202) 482-5081
Web site: http://www.doc.gov/eda

Department of Housing and Urban Development
451 Seventh Street, S.W.
Washington, DC 20410
(202) 708-1420
Web site: http://www.hud.gov

Department of the Interior
Bureau of Indian Affairs
1849 C Street N.W.
Washington, DC 20240
(202) 208-5116
Web site: http://www.doi.gov/bureau-indian-affairs.html

Department of Treasury
Community Development Financial Institutions Fund
601 Thirteenth Street, N.W., Suite 200 South
Washington, DC 20005
(202) 622-8662
Web site: http://www.cdfifund.gov

Department of Treasury
Financial Management Service
Cash Management Policy and Planning
401 - 14th Street, S.W., Room 420
Washington, DC 20227
(202) 874-6590
Web site: http://www.treas.gov/fms/cashmanagement/index.html

Department of Treasury
Financial Crimes Enforcement Network (FINCEN)
2070 Chain Bridge Road
Vienna, Virginia 22181
(703) 905-3591
Web site: http://www.treas.gov/fincen

Internal Revenue Service
Federal Low Income Housing Tax Credits
11601 Roosevelt Blvd.
(ATTN: DP8235-607)
Philadelphia, Pennsylvania 19255
(215) 516-4113
Web site: http://www.irs.gov

Small Business Administration
Information Office, Office of Advocacy
409 Third Street, S.W.
Washington, DC 20416
(202) 205-6531
Web site: http://www.sba.gov

Department of Veterans Affairs
Veterans Benefits Administration
810 Vermont Avenue, N.W.
Washington, DC 20420
(202) 273-7481
Web site: http://www.vba.va.gov

National Housing Intermediaries

Corporation for Supportive Housing
50 Broadway, 17th Floor
New York, NewYork 10004
(212) 986-2966
Web site: http://www.csh.org

The Enterprise Foundation
American City Building
10227 Wincopin Circle, Suite 500
Columbia, Maryland 21044-3400
(410) 964-1230
Web site: http://www.enterprisefoundation.org

Family Housing Fund
801 Nicollet Mall, Suite 1840
Minneapolis, Minnesota 55402
(612) 375-9644
Web site: http://www.fhfund.org

Housing Assistance Council
1025 Vermont Avenue, N.W.
Washington, DC 20005
(202) 842-8600
Web site: http://www.ruralhome.org

Local Initiatives Support Corporation
1825 K Street, N.W., Suite 1100
Washington, DC 20006
(202) 785-2908
Web site: http://www.liscnet.org

National Association of Affordable Housing Lenders
2121 K Street, NW, Suite 700
Washington, DC 20037
(202) 293-9850
Web site: http://www.ffhsj.com/fairlending/naahl.htm

Neighborhood Reinvestment Corporation
1325 G Street, N.W., Suite 800
Washington, DC 20005
(202) 220-2300
Web site: http://www.nw.org/network/home.asp

Secondary Market Resources

Fannie Mae
3900 Wisconsin Avenue, N.W.
Washington, DC 20016
(202) 752-7000
Web site: http://www.fanniemae.com

Federal Agricultural Mortgage Corporation (Farmer Mac)
1133 21st Street, N.W., Suite 600
Washington, DC 20036
(800) 879-3276
Web site: http://www.farmermac.com/plane/frames.htm

Federal Home Loan Mortgage Corporation (Freddie Mac)
8200 Jones Branch Drive
McLean, Virginia 22102
(703) 903-4000
Web site: http://www.freddiemac.com

Government National Mortgage Association (Ginnie Mae)
Department of Housing and Urban Development
451 Seventh Street, S.W.
Washington, DC 20410
(202) 708-0926
Web site: http://www.ginniemae.gov

Federal Financial Regulators — Community Affairs Contacts

Office of the Comptroller of the Currency
Anna Alvarez Boyd, Deputy Comptroller, Community Affairs
250 E Street, S.W.
Washington, DC 20219-0001
(202) 874-5864
Web site: http://www.occ.treas.gov

Board of Governors, Federal Reserve System
Sandra Braunstein, Assistant Director and Community Affairs Officer
20th and Constitution Avenue, N.W.
Washington, DC 20551
(202) 452-3378
Web site: http://www.bog.frb.fed.us

Federal Deposit Insurance Corporation
George French, Deputy Director for Supervision and Consumer Protection
550 17th Street, N.W.
Washington, DC 20429
(202) 898-3929
Web site: http://www.fdic.gov

Federal Housing Finance Board
Stephen Hudak, Director of Communications
1777 F Street, N.W.
Washington, DC 20006
(202) 408-2807
Web site: http://www.fhfb.gov

National Credit Union Administration
Anthony LaCreta, Director, Office of Community Development Credit Unions
1775 Duke Street
Alexandria, Virginia 22314-3428
(703) 518-6610
Web site: http://www.ncua.gov

Office of Thrift Supervision
U.S. Department of Treasury
Sonja White, National Community Affairs Liaison
1700 G Street, N.W.
Washington, DC 20552
(202) 906-7857
Web site: http://www.ots.gov

Glossary of Terms

Acting in concert means knowingly participating in a joint activity or parallel action toward a common goal of acquiring control, whether or not pursuant to an express agreement. It also can mean combining voting or other interests for a common purpose in any contract, understanding, relationship, agreement, or other arrangement whether or not written.

An **applicant** is a person or entity that submits a notice or application to the OCC.

An **application** is a submission requesting prior OCC approval to engage in various corporate activities or transactions (also see **notice** definition).

A **community development corporation (CDC)** is a corporation established by one or more insured financial institutions, or by insured financial institutions and other investors, to make one or more investments that meet the public welfare investment requirements of 12 CFR 24.2(c).

A certified **community development entity** is an organization that is certified by the CDFI Fund as being eligible to receive tax credits under the New Markets Tax Credits program.

A **community development financial institution** (CDFI) is a financial institution that specializes in serving underserved communities and the people who live there. CDFIs include community development banks, credit unions, loan funds, microenterprise loan funds, venture capital funds, and multibank CDCs.

A **community development project (CD Project)** is a project to make an investment that meets the public welfare investment requirements of 12 CFR 24.2(d).

A **corporate filing** or **filing** is either an application or a notice.

The **Community Reinvestment Act regulations** establish the framework and criteria by which the federal financial regulators assess a financial institution's record of helping to meet the credit needs of the financial institution's community (12 CFR 25).

A **depository institution** is a financial institution that accepts deposits.

A **filer** is a person, group of persons, national bank, state-chartered bank, thrift, other financial institution, or any other entity that submits a corporate filing to the OCC.

Holding company means any company that controls or proposes to control a national bank regardless of whether it is a bank holding company under 12 USC 1841(a)(1).

An **incomplete filing** is not fully responsive to each item of information included in a sample notice or application or lacks adequate information, when considered together with other available information, for the OCC to make its decision.

An **Indian** or **Native American**, for most governmental and jurisdictional purposes, is a person (a) of Indian descent and (b) an enrolled member of a federally recognized Indian tribe. Those terms are used interchangeably in this guide.

Indian country is defined by Congress as land inside the boundaries of Indian reservations, communities made up mainly of Indians, and Indian trust and restricted land.[1]

An **Indian tribe** is a "domestic dependent nation"[2] with governmental authority over its members and its territory. It has a unique legal and government-to-government relationship with the United States that is reflected in the United States Constitution, treaties, statutes, and court decisions. Under federal law, the Secretary of the Interior maintains a list of Indian tribes that are recognized by the United States as governments.[3]

An **insider** is a proposed organizer, director, principal shareholder, or executive officer of a proposed or existing national bank and includes any related interest of such a person.

An **insider contract** is any financial or other business, voting, or ownership agreement, arrangement, or transaction, direct or indirect, oral or written, between any insider and the proposed bank.

An **institution-affiliated party** (IAP)[4] may include:

---

[1] 18 USC 1151.

[2] Cherokee Nation v. Georgia, 30 U.S. (5 Pet.) 1, 17 (1831).

[3] "Indian Entities Recognized and Eligible to Receive Services from the United States Bureau of Indian Affairs," 67 Fed. Reg. 46,328 (July 12, 2002).

[4] 12 USC 1813(u).

- A director, officer, employee, or controlling shareholder of an insured depository institution.

- A person who has filed or is required to file a change in bank control notice under 12 USC 1817(j).

- Any shareholder, consultant, joint venture partner, or other person, who participates in the conduct of the affairs of an insured depository institution.

- Any independent contractor who knowingly or recklessly participates in any violation of a law or regulation, any breach of fiduciary duty, or any unsafe or unsound practice, which caused or is likely to cause more than a minimal financial loss to, or a significant adverse effect on, the insured depository institution.

An **interim bank** is a non-operational bank chartered solely to merge or consolidate into another bank owned by the same party.

A **loan pool** is formed when two or more financial institutions simultaneously agree to commit a fixed dollar amount of loans or loan participations for a particular community development purpose or geographical target area. Often, each individual institution originates loans by using borrower eligibility criteria and loan rates, terms, and conditions agreed to by all bank participants. In some cases, one institution serves as the lender of record and other banks agree to purchase participations in each loan made under the program. In other instances, borrowers seeking financing from the pool will be referred to lenders on a revolving basis, so that each bank takes a turn originating loans. Often, local development agencies receive the loan requests and may provide loan packaging assistance.

For the Minority Bank Deposit Program (MBDP), the term **minority control** applies when minority persons own or control more than 50 percent of the outstanding voting stock of a financial institution.

A **minority depository institution** is a depository institution with more than 50 percent of the ownership or control held by one or more minority individuals, and more than 50 percent of the net profit or loss of which accrues to minority individuals. The term **"minority"** means any Black American, Native American, Hispanic American, or Asian American (12 USC 1823(f)(12)(B)).

Money laundering is the movement of criminally derived funds to conceal the true source, ownership, or use of the funds.

A **multibank lending corporation** is a corporate structure that originates community development loans on behalf of members or stockholders. Although many variations in structure exist, participating financial institutions typically may provide:

- Direct loans to businesses or projects in which the loans are pre-packaged by the corporation.

- Revolving lines of credit to the corporation that are drawn down as loans made by the corporation.

- Purchase of participations in loans originated by the corporation.

Usually, professional staff manages these entities with bankers serving on the board of directors and on the loan review committee.

A **notice** is a submission notifying the OCC that a filer: (1) intends to engage in certain corporate activities or transactions; or, (2) has begun certain corporate activities or transactions (see also **application** definition).

Anti-Money Laundering Provisions
    Laws   18 USC 1956, 1957
                                         31 USC 5311 et seq.
    Regulation   31 CFR 103

Appeals Process
    Regulation   12 CFR 5.13(f)
    OCC Issuance   OCC 96-18

Bank Enterprise Act
    Law   12 USC 1834a
    Regulation   12 CFR 1806

Bank Holding Company Act
    Law   12 USC 1841 et seq.

Bank Merger Act
    Law   12 USC 1828(c)
    Regulation   12 CFR 5.33

Bank Secrecy Act
    Law   31 USC 5311 et seq.
    Regulations   31 CFR 103
                                         12 CFR 21.21

Branches
    Law   12 USC 36
    Regulation   12 CFR 5.30

Change in Bank Control Act
    Law   12 USC 1817(j)
    Regulation   12 CFR 5.50

Community Development Financial Institutions
    Law   12 USC 4701 et seq.
    Regulation   12 CFR 1805

Community Development Investments
    Law   12 USC 24(11)
    Regulation   12 CFR 24

Community Reinvestment Act
Law   12 USC 2901 et seq.
Regulation   12 CFR 25

Corporate Decisions
Laws   12 USC 93a, 1818(b),
                1831o(e)(4)
Regulation   12 CFR 5.13

Corporate Definitions
Regulation   12 CFR 5.3

Equal Credit Opportunity Act
Law   15 USC 1691 et seq.
Regulation   12 CFR 202

Fair Housing Act
Law   42 USC 3601 et seq.
Regulation   24 CFR 100

Federal Deposit Insurance Act
Law   12 USC 1811 et seq.

Federal Reserve Act
Law   12 USC 221 et seq.

Filing Fees
Regulation   12 CFR 5.5

Hearings and Other Meetings
Regulation   12 CFR 5.11

Interstate Branching
Law   12 USC 36
Regulation   12 CFR 5.30

Loans to Insiders
Regulations   12 CFR 31, 215

Misrepresentations or Omissions
Law   18 USC 1001

National Bank Act
Law   12 USC 1 et seq.

Public Comment
Regulation   12 CFR 5.10

Public File Availability
Regulation   12 CFR 5.9

Publication Requirement
Regulation   12 CFR 5.8

Restrictions on Transactions with Affiliates
Laws   12 USC 371c (Section 23A),
                                              371c-1 (Section 23B)
Regulation   12 CFR 31, various provisions
                                              in 12 CFR part 250

Securities
Regulations   12 CFR 11, 16

Small Business Investment Companies (SBICs)
Law   15 USC 681 et seq.

Tribal Relationships
Presidential memorandum dated April 29, 1994, for the heads of
executive departments and agencies, "Government-to-Government
Relations with Native American Tribal Governments," 59 Fed. Reg.
22,951 (May 4, 1994).

Executive Order No. 13175 on "Consultation and Coordination with
Indian Tribal Governments," 65 Fed. Reg. 67,249 (November 9, 2000).